The Story of Toronto

The Story of Toronto

Through the Lives of
John and Carol Arnott

John Peters

Authentic

British Library Cataloguing in Publication Data
A catalogue record for this book is available from the
British Library.

ISBN 1-85078-647-X

Cover Design by fourninezero design.
Typeset by Textype Typesetters, Cambridge

Contents

Dedication

This book is dedicated to my wife Elisabeth and my three children, Daniel, Kathie and Joanna, for their unfailing love and unstinting encouragement.

Acknowledgements

I wish to record my gratitude to a number of people – without their cooperation this book would not have been possible. I am particularly grateful to John and Carol Arnott who not only gave me permission to write this account, but who did not interfere at any stage in the conclusions I reached. In addition, Lori and Vicky (John's daughters), who willingly granted me lengthy interviews in Toronto and were invaluable in painting a picture of their family life; Jeremy and Connie Sinnott, Steve Long, Peter and Heather Jackson, Ian Ross, David Campbell, Colin Dye and Jeff Duncan too deserve thanks for responding to my many questions. I deeply appreciate Dr R.T. Kendall's generosity in writing a foreword to the book. Lastly, Sheila Jacobs edited my manuscript with meticulous care and rigorous attention to detail, thus saving me from many errors. All imperfections in this work are, of course, my responsibility.

Foreword

Many of us have been waiting for a book like this. Though long over due, it is worth waiting for. I am honoured to be invited to write this foreword. I know John and Carol Arnott personally, invited them to minister in Westminster Chapel when I was there, and have worked with them a number of times since on both sides of the Atlantic. What follows is a lively and gripping biography of John and Carol themselves, as well as an account of their ministry which is now ongoing all over the world.

John Peters has done a brilliant piece of work in providing an objective picture of what began in Toronto in 1994 – known to all as the 'Toronto Blessing'. Whereas he obviously is writing as one who is no enemy to this work of the Spirit, he nonetheless keeps his promise to bring us a 'realistic assessment' of what has happened through the lives and ministries of John and Carol Arnott. John Peters bestowed upon the church generally an enormous favour and will, as much as one could reasonably expect, disarm and diffuse the critics of this phenomenon. Vindication as such is never promised until the Second Coming (2 Thes. 1:6,7), and none of us will ever outgrow persecution. But those who have affirmed the Toronto Blessing, as I have, will be gratified that this volume has finally come forth.

I am probably not the first, and certainly won't be the last, to call John Arnott the 'gentle bear'. This is the way I have seen him from the start: so laid back, so gracious and unpretentious. But he seldom ministers alone. God must love him a lot because he gave John his lovely Carol to be at his side – supporting him, working with him with an equivalent anointing, and blessing all who get in her path with the ministry of laying on of hands. It is a thrill to see them working together, but the next best thing is to read this book! You will not be able to put it down.

When I invited John Arnott to preach at Westminster Chapel (the only time I ever saw him in a suit!), I never felt so inwardly affirmed by the Holy Spirit for endorsing his ministry. His preaching on forgiveness on that Sunday morning exceeded anything I myself have said on a subject that is dear to my heart. I thought 'how could anybody criticise this man?' but when manifestations like those associated with John and Carol's ministry spring forth, we are taken right out of our comfort zones – and we look for ways to defend ourselves.

The title of this book, *Giving Away the Love of God*, is apt for the Arnotts' ministry. John Peters has shown that this is literally all John and Carol want to do! They have not held on to it for themselves, they have not tried to keep it in Toronto; they have done all within their power to share the Father's love to the world. This in my opinion is largely why this extraordinary move of the Spirit has not died down. They knew if they tried to hoard it in any way, they would indeed lose it. They have kept giving it away. However, the unsung heroes of this story are those precious members of the Toronto Christian Fellowship who have tirelessly come to the church night after night for years and years to pray for people. It shows their devotion and respect for John and Carol. But we must never forget those people who have been self-effacing and faithful in their ministries of laying on of hands to tens of thousands of people from all over the world.

Louise and I were in the Toronto church a few weeks ago (January 2005). I can safely report that the wave of the Holy Spirit in this church is as real and potent as ever. I observed and felt the presence of the Holy Spirit – it seemed exactly the same as when I first visited the church in 1996. There are not many places in the world where, while being there, I want to pinch myself that I am where I am – like being in London or Jerusalem. But I always got that feeling in the Toronto church, whenever I was privileged to be there. This church has passed on to the world what I continue to regard as the embryonic phase of what will eventually be seen as the greatest work of the Spirit since the days of the earliest church. It is only the beginning.

May the Holy Spirit witness to you personally as you read what follows, and I pray it will change your life as it has thousands and thousands of others, as well as those in my own family. And may God receive great honour and glory from the book John Peters has written for us all.

R.T. Kendall
Key Largo, Florida
8 March 2005

Chapter One

Introduction

John and Carol Arnott, senior pastors at the Toronto Airport Christian Fellowship (TACF), are ordinary, unpretentious people. Totally devoid of airs and graces, they are, in private conversation, friendly and unassuming. Neither seeks to impress people by their charisma or their achievements, but they do invariably impress other people with the humility, integrity and genuineness of their character. The reasons for this impression are because they are two people who, throughout their Christian lives, have built into their experience levels of character and openness that are much more impressive than any showy demonstration of sophistication or style or knowledge.

Today they are known throughout the Christian world – not always approvingly in some quarters – as the leaders of what has become known as the 'Toronto Blessing', a moniker they themselves do not use, preferring instead 'The Father's Blessing'. The inescapable fact is that this global dimension would not be present or so active a part of their ministry were it not for the tumultuous events of refreshing and renewal that broke out on 20 January 1994, and which continue robustly without any indication of waning or losing impetus at the present time. Both were surprised, though welcomed whole-heartedly, the powerful demonstration of the Holy Spirit that occurred that night, and they continue to be amazed that the Spirit continues to work so dynamically in their church and in their ministry around the world.

So 20 January 1994 is by far the most significant date in the comparatively brief history of TACF, formerly known as the Toronto Airport Vineyard (TAV). It is considered by some (Dr Mark Stibbe, the Anglican clergyman included) to be an important, even seminal landmark, in the history of the Christian Church in the twentieth-century.[1] Other commentators are persuaded that one day the history books will point to the Toronto outpouring as the precursor to authentic revival in the western world as a whole. Whether that will be the case is, as yet, unproven, though global revival remains the yearning of many thousands of Christians throughout the world, a longing that John and Carol passionately share, and which in John's case particularly is sharpened by a keen interest in the history of past revivals, especially the Welsh Revival 1904–05.

Two facts, however, are indisputable. First, that the events of that tumultuous Thursday night and what followed subsequently totally transformed what had previously been an obscure church nestling at the end of the bustling international airport in Toronto and housed in a distinctly unimpressive (and noisy!) building. All too easily the phrase 'life-changing' is used in Christian circles, but it is appropriately applied to TACF, both for the local church there and also for so many people who subsequently visited it. Second, that a worldwide movement has emanated from Toronto bringing with it refreshing and renewal in creative and exciting ways. Colin Dye, senior pastor at Kensington Temple, probably the largest church in Britain, has expressed this forthright opinion: 'the Toronto Blessing is the most significant movement since the Pentecostal movement at the start of the twentieth century'.[2] High praise indeed when the effect of the Pentecostal movement is pondered.

The 1994 outbreak inevitably raised questions and queries in the Christian – and even the secular – press, including 'why Toronto?' and 'what's the nature of the blessing anyway?' To the first of these queries John Arnott's laconic, seemingly casual, reply was 'because it's near an airport.' More directly confrontational approaches – though perfectly reasonable, given the ferment and discussion it caused – were to ask if the

Toronto phenomenon is, indeed, a blessing and, more fundamentally, if it is biblical. Others have wondered whether an experience is appropriately deemed to be biblical.

In this context, David Pawson, a highly respected evangelical teacher and preacher in Britain, has pointed to the inter-relationship between a desire for a fresh, dynamic, ongoing experience of the Holy Spirit, on the one hand, and the plumb-line of the Scriptures as the indispensable guide to Christian ideals of sacrifice, service and servanthood, on the other. A summary of his material may be put in the form of two questions we shall come back to several times in this book: (1) is the Toronto Blessing really the work of the Holy Spirit? And (2) is it the end-time revival countless thousands of Christians have longed for that will halt the manifest decline of both church and society? Pawson is not entirely convinced on either issue, and the general perspective of his book is perhaps summed up by its title: *Is the 'Blessing' Biblical?*[3] His questions are penetrating and pastoral, blending both wisdom and criticism, although his comments are possibly muted by the fact that he has not visited Toronto to see, at first hand, what goes on there. However, his book raises a number of issues that need to be addressed.

Media attention – especially in the two or three years immediately following January 1994 – was both intense and huge, with every aspect of the phenomenon, initially in Canada and then throughout the world, being subjected to comprehensive analysis, with many Christian leaders rushing into print with accounts of their 'experiences' and the palpable benefits they derived (or not) either from visiting Toronto itself or attending Toronto-style meetings.

Leaders came from all the major denominations, as indeed did those who opposed strongly, even virulently, what Toronto stood for and the core values it espoused and represented. Sociological studies, theological critiques and denunciations followed fairly rapidly, often dividing predictably along particular denominational lines.

One British leader, David Matthews, senior pastor of New Harvest Community Church in Brentwood, Essex, England, sees Toronto as a place of pilgrimage where the presence of

God was powerfully and tangibly felt, and for him the whole experience was beneficial, and hugely encouraging.[4] Matthews asked himself why he had to go to Toronto, thinking perfectly properly that God could touch him at home in England, with significant saving of both air fare and time. He resolved the issue by recalling the Christmas story: 'It seems as if there is a part of God that longs to be localised. Down through church history God has "contracted" Himself to certain people and places. When he does that He invites those who wish to make pilgrimage.' In personal terms, Matthews also received inner healing, 'the last part of a process whereby I was freed from long-standing depression that was growing worse as I was growing older.' Equally significantly, given the core teaching at TACF, he rediscovered 'the Father's heart', which changed his view of how 'we treat one another and also how to relate to those who are not yet Christians.'

It is also important to point to the fact that countless thousands of 'ordinary' Christians have made the pilgrimage to Toronto, where they have much appreciated the ministry of John and Carol Arnott in particular, and the whole experience of renewal.

Julia Ackroyd, of Maidstone, Kent, England, is one such person, and she records her impressions of Toronto and the Arnotts in the following way: 'Their ministry and passion for Jesus has blessed my life very much. My husband [Gerald] and I were in Toronto for the first time in October 1995. We had been through years of family problems, which had come to a head that year. I hadn't realised just how much I had erected barriers against God in my life and kept him at arm's length, in spite of having known a measure of his blessing. After the very first renewal meeting that we attended at TACF, Carol Arnott prayed for me and, after this, I remember lying on the carpet in floods of tears. Later that night, back in our hotel, I woke up with a very strong sense of inner burning, and I felt as if the Lord's words were streaming through my heart. I felt that he spoke to me about returning to intimacy with himself, that he wanted to draw me to his heart, of compassion and understanding, and that when I was hurting, to turn to him and not away from him. He gave me this sense of his unconditional love, and it was as if he cut through the barriers, bound me to himself and lit a flame inside me that night that has increased with the passage of time.'

What Julia understood was that God wants to give all Christians a revelation of his heart, and also that he is currently restoring his bride to beauty. She also said this: 'I am so thankful to John and Carol for their faithfulness in making a place for the Holy Spirit to come in gentleness and healing, and to draw people, often really hurting people, into a depth of intimacy with Jesus that they have never known before. John and Carol so model the Father's heart and the love of Jesus, in their lives and in their teaching and ministry.'

At the time of Julia's first visit to Toronto she had been a Christian for over forty years, but her sense of gratitude is palpable in her comments. What happened was that she came into a fresh understanding of the Father's love and passion for his people, of the church as the bride of Christ, and of the Holy Spirit's gentle, healing and restorative love. In addition, as she also wrote in the same letter, the whole experience led to a transformation of love in her marriage with Gerald and with her immediate family. From another perspective, it is clear that the experience for Julia was not theoretical or outlandish or weird, rather it was gentle, encouraging, albeit challenging, and had its outworking in practical ways, both in terms of Christian understanding and behaviour, and in several personal ways too.

Another most instructive perspective is provided by Lucille Lambert, of Bermuda, who identifies the influence of the Toronto Blessing and the ministry of John and Carol in the following way. 'From John's mouth I began to hear with my heart that God loves me. Father God used both John and Carol to relate the good news in such a matter-of-fact way that's so simple it persuades one to believe – it is disarming. Each time I hear John talk about God's love and Jesus I feel refreshed like someone shared something precious with me on a one-to-one basis. I no longer feel that I have been the victim of an "oration attack" and that the preacher has got it together and I had better get it real quick. I visited the TACF around 1994, I believe, and was comforted by the fact that John Arnott as leader of the church allowed people the freedom to react and not to stifle what was happening. I saw some groups who I felt were obviously just plain having fun in this freedom. [They] began in me a process of dismantling the yoke of religion I had been under for too many years. I felt that TACF was a safe place for people to learn to come to a loving Father. I am still working these ideas out in my personal and church lives.' Lucille's feelings are shared by thousands of other ordinary people.

The experiences of Julia and Lucille are valuable ones to record, but there can be no denying, however, that the Toronto phenomenon was – and is – viewed as something controversial. Indeed, in a scholarly, careful and highly respected publication, *'Toronto' in Perspective,*[5] sponsored by ACUTE, the Evangelical Alliance Commission on Unity and Truth Among Evangelicals, the word 'crisis' is used in relation to the Toronto outworking. As the editor, David Hilborn, helpfully explains, the word crisis has a double meaning: judgement and opportunity. In his view, the whole concept of crisis can, in fact, teach salutary lessons, suggesting fresh possibilities, and can be turned to constructive ends; and he sees the Toronto Blessing 'not so much for what it was in and of itself, but for what it revealed about the state of evangelical and charismatic Christianity at the turn of the Millennium.'

Hilborn's perspective is a most helpful and constructive starting-point. It certainly appears to be more balanced and objective than the opinions of Alan Morrison[6] who characterises the whole Toronto phenomenon as 'at best, the out-workings of a childish and hysterical mimicry; at worst, they are the result of something more sinister'. What he means by 'something more sinister' is not easy to determine; his views seem to suggest that the leaders in Toronto have an agenda to mimic and somehow manipulate the Holy Spirit, which is not the understanding of anyone who has had personal contact and acquaintance with John and Carol Arnott. Incidentally the history of Christianity shows that movements or revivals cannot be manipulated into existence. Alan Morrison's views, however, have one valuable function: they cause men and women who have experienced, at first hand, the effects of the Toronto Blessing, to reassess the issue for themselves.

One such person is Mike Fearon, who wrote a swift and robust response to what was happening at TACF and around the world. In *A Breath of Fresh Air*, he judiciously allows his readers to make up their own minds by saying this: 'The blessing either is or isn't a powerful outpouring of God's Spirit. If it is, and the manifestations appear to be contrary to God's received word in the Scriptures, then either God is wrong, or the critic's theology is wrong, and needs urgently to be reassessed'.[7] That's the bottom line.

But how did this book come to be written? A word of explanation might be helpful at this point. The author was converted in 1955, after which point he was privileged to worship with the Open Brethren (where he particularly appreciated their insistence on the absolute trustworthiness of Scripture in all matters of faith, belief and conduct) and various charismatic churches (where he particularly welcomed their openness to the ongoing work and freedom of the Holy Spirit, both in terms of fruit and gifts). He also had a life-transforming experience when he received the baptism of the Holy Spirit.

In addition, eight visits to Toronto have given the author abundant opportunities for perusing, directly and at first hand, TACF itself, its leaders and various conferences there, as well as attending Toronto-style meetings in Britain. Tapes, videos and other media publications have helped in establishing and honing some of the material in this volume. It also includes some reflection, in the light of the Scriptures, on a movement that cannot be airily dismissed (as some do) as being either of no consequence or of being totally deluded. Presumably four million-plus visitors to Toronto (between 1994–2004) can't all be deceived.

Inevitably the material relating to the Toronto Blessing has reached significant proportions, but amidst the plethora of books and articles available a gap is discernible. It is that very little has been written biographically about John and Carol Arnott, a gap this volume seeks to address. They both seem to have avoided hagiography (which is largely redundant in terms of realistic assessment anyway), on the one hand, and character assassination, on the other hand, which is equally unproductive and unhelpful in approaching the whole question.

What reasons explain this surprising gap? The answer to this question is directly related to the sort of people they are. They are not motivated by fame and media exposure, rather by a fixed and insistent desire, in the words of the huge banner at the back of TACF, to 'give away the love of God, first to Toronto, then to the world'. This desire really does consume all their energies. Another contributory factor is their innately modest lifestyle, both at home and also when travelling abroad: no personal jets, or exotic cars, or five star hotels for them; in contrast, one is tempted to remark, to many high-profile Christian ministries in the contemporary Christian world. They carry about them a sort of naivety, being genuinely surprised (in 1994 and ten years on) by the way God has used them. Quite simply they attribute everything solely to God's grace and love. But while they do not court publicity, they are, within the confines of the Christian world, 'famous', though this does not interest them at all, and certainly they are highly respected wherever they travel in the world.

The genesis of this book may be traced back to July 2001 when the author interviewed John Arnott in his study at TACF in preparation for a projected article for *Revival World Report*, then a bi-monthly magazine published by Crusade for World Revival. A year later this was followed by a tentative suggestion of a longer, more comprehensive study, which received John's gentle if rather casual encouragement. Another year elapsed before a more formal suggestion was made regarding a possible biography, which John and Carol agreed to. So, as it is written with their active cooperation, it carries the imprimatur of an authorised biography. Central to the whole book is the author's contention that theirs is a story worth telling, not least for future historians of late twentieth and early twenty-first century Christianity. For this reason too, biographical and interpretive material on the Arnotts have been placed against several conceptual aspects of revival and renewal.

Since January 1994, John and Carol have presided over enormous numbers in their own church, handled a complex administrative system catering for hundreds of thousands of visitors, in addition to which they travel extensively each year, often as much as a hundred days in locations all over the world. They also direct 'The Partners in Harvest' which seeks to link and encourage churches who share their core values. John explained the reasons for such a network in this way: 'I realised after talking to several leaders in the body of Christ that all of us have a need for our churches and ministries to have an identity as well as a desire to belong to something bigger than ourselves. We are [also] able to share resources with one another and strengthen each other's hand in many and varied ways.' This network now embraces churches and ministries in at least thirty countries around the world, with the majority being located in America, Canada and the United Kingdom. Is such a grouping a denomination? John's answer is direct and straightforward: 'If a denomination means an identifying name for a specific family in the broader church, then we are. If denomination refers to conformity to a tight pattern of insisting on firm control, then we are not.' Ultimately 'Partners in Harvest' is a pursuit of renewal and revival, which are at the very heart of John and Carol's ministry.

To fully appreciate the changes that occurred in the wake of January 1994, one only has to compare the very ordinary premises at Dixie Road (situated at the end of a runway of the Toronto international airport and which was engulfed in noise when huge aeroplanes took off or landed) with the multi-media facilities, including television, available at 275 Attwell Drive, the current home of TACF, which was purchased for just over two million Canadian dollars. John and Carol rightly view the purchase of these premises as something of a 'miracle' (John's word) because at the time of the proposed purchase the church was distinctly short of money.

More significantly, they were jettisoned into a sharp learning curve, and Steve Hepden captures something of their changed circumstances in his account of a meeting in May 1994

> There were people there from all over the world. Of course, there were many from the USA and Canada, but it seemed that, at some of the meetings, there were more present from the UK than

anywhere else. The place was heaving by the time the meeting started and the praise and worship took off . . . It was as though the world knew something was happening [and] all sorts of people were turning up.[8]

Such vast crowds did though constitute a problem for John and Carol, just in purely organisational terms. They needed wisdom to bring godly order and discipline into what seemed a confused and chaotic situation without, at the same time, quenching the operation of the Holy Spirit. The dilemma for them was how to bring a proper sense of authority which complemented – and facilitated – the refreshing and renewal of the Spirit.

John and Carol's lives and ministry are inextricably linked to the Toronto Blessing, and the material that follows is structured thematically so as to reflect this fact. Of primary concern is the occasion in January 1994 that led to such a dynamic outpouring in TACF. It is important too to reflect on the way their lives were shaped up to that point. In addition, important biographical details will be given, together with perspectives gleaned from an exhaustive number of interviews with people who have worked with them, or have more generally encountered them in their public ministry, or who know them as friends. What will emerge – hardly surprisingly perhaps – is that their lives, like most men and women, are a mosaic of the sad and the happy, the victorious and the defeated, the humorous and the serious. Their personal values and qualities will also be examined, the inescapable conclusion being that for John and Carol Arnott character is much more important and certainly more long-lasting that the merely superficial aspects of charismatic life and witness. They constantly stress the imperative of 'good fruit' in the lives of Christian men and women (Gal. 5:22,23): God is looking not for silky external skills but for right attitudes of heart leading to behaviour appropriate to the Christian faith, and which is intimately linked to the life of God flowing through individual lives. Something of these twin emphases is encapsulated in the following poem, by Crispin Hill, which was inspired by John Arnott's teaching in *Spread the Fire* (Issue 5, 2003)

Give time in silent worship till My love
Can drench your very being from above.

I yearn to be so intimate with you
That I can share your joy, your whole life through.

So, in the silence, let My still small voice
Speak total reassurance, and rejoice.

My joy's to fill you with My Spirit's power
And warm your heart with each quiet hour.

Give time, and let My precious life-blood flow
And speak your mind and spirit till you glow

And feel My tender closeness, passing wonder,
Which, from your life, no foe can tear asunder.

But, as any balanced understanding of the lives of John and Carol must begin with reference to the exciting events of January 1994, it is to those happenings we turn in the next chapter.

Chapter Two

The Event

This was, as is obvious by now, the meeting on Thursday, 20 January 1994. The day itself was typical of mid-winter Toronto: crisply cold, with only thin and meagre wisps of sun piercing ineffectually through the invigorating cold. Nothing unusual about the weather and the climate, and apparently nothing unusual had been arranged either: it all seemed fairly routine and uncomplicated in the ongoing life of TACF (known as Toronto Airport Vineyard at the time), a church that had been established less than ten years earlier. The church was then housed in what can only be described as a poor industrial building with inadequate parking facilities. It was noisy, not particularly comfortable, and certainly inappropriate for a huge influx of visitors. Nor did John and Carol have significant expectations of the scheduled programme ahead of them.

Randy Clark, a casual friend of the Arnotts, the founding pastor of the Vineyard Christian Fellowship in St Louis, Missouri, had been invited to be the guest speaker. The invitation had come about because John had heard of various supernatural events at a mid-west regional meeting of the Vineyard grouping of churches, in Wisconsin. Signs and wonders had apparently accompanied the preaching of the word. Randy was at first understandably cautious, warning John that simply because powerful events had taken place in Wisconsin did not mean that they would also occur in Toronto. Arnott persisted, the additional request being that Clark should preach four times. He protested, 'I can't preach four times. All I have is a testimony and one sermon,' adding: 'I can bring my assistant, and he can preach to your kids and to the youth. We'll stay four nights, and then we'll come. OK?' John readily agreed, while Randy remained nervous about the whole project, which was to involve a family night on the Thursday, a children's meeting on the Friday, a meeting for the youth and adults on the Saturday, followed by regular (Vineyard) worship on Sunday.

The scheduled meetings as arranged by John, and agreed with Randy, were uncomplicated and consistent with their normal services: worship, testimonies, then a biblical exposition. These three activities are the 'golden threads' of the Arnotts' public ministry, because John has always subscribed to the view that the preaching of the word of God is invariably most effective and far-reaching when based unequivocally on worship; an activity the late A.W. Tozer described as a 'privilege to wonder, to stand in delighted silence before the Supreme Mystery'[9], and John has always placed a high value on men and women testifying to what God has done and achieved in their lives. Christianity to him is not a matter of bland theory or cold logical norms, nor is it book knowledge or something divorced from the realities and often the tragedies of everyday life. Faith, to him inculcates both belief and practice, demonstrating not only the biblical verities, but a practical outworking of belief in the manner advocated in the teaching of the New Testament.

John and Carol, whilst looking forward to the preaching of Randy Clark, did not have the slightest inkling of what lay ahead. Nor were they, self-admittedly, full of faith and confident expectation. On the other hand, Randy Clark and his team, in prayerful preparation beforehand, had been given a vision of a map with 'fire breaking out in Toronto then burning up the whole map.'

Randy's preaching had often been accompanied by outpourings of the Holy Spirit's power, but he shared with John Arnott an uncertainty about what happened in the meetings. There was another dimension too: the regular worshippers at Dixie Road were not particularly girded with faith either, but God was about to increase their faith levels dramatically. In fact, he was about to disrupt the agreed programme and, in John's own words, 'fulfil the vision of the Toronto map in a most unusual and powerful manner.' One personal side-effect for Randy Clark, somewhat to his wife's bemusement, was that he spent forty-two of the next sixty days in Toronto, and he has, of course, returned on a number of occasions since then, including the tenth 'Catch The Fire' conference in October 2003. In the event, the outpouring did not resemble or conform to any conceptions or preconceived ideas the Arnotts may have entertained about renewal or revival. In reality, their expectations were rather limited and narrow, as John admits honestly: 'We had been praying for God to move, and our assumption was we would see more people saved and healed, along with the excitement that it would generate.' There was, of course, nothing wrong or misguided about wanting men and women to be saved and healed – they are, after all, normative, biblical expectations, and when they occur in significant numbers, as in the Acts of the Apostles for example, they inevitably generate excitement and a marked increase in the levels of faith. John's words probably represented his personal faith at that juncture in his ministry. So what happened? What was the event now known by the emotively charged words 'The Toronto Blessing' that has caused such ripples throughout the Christian world?

Put at its most prosaic level, the meetings arranged for Friday, Saturday and Sunday did not take place as envisaged and as agreed between John Arnott and Randy Clark. The Holy Spirit intervened not only to disrupt the scheduled programme, but to set in motion an outworking and a refreshing that continues today. Another side-effect was to propel Randy into a worldwide ministry that also continues to operate powerfully to this day, combining real concern for the poor and the under-privileged with the supernatural operation of the gifts of the Holy Spirit.

At the end of his preaching (it is tempting to ask if this was the one message he claimed to have when in conversation earlier with John), Randy Clark invited the congregation – estimates vary from a hundred and twenty to a hundred and sixty – to come forward for prayer. Almost everyone responded, an unusual and surprising fact in itself, though that wasn't all that occurred.

A range of manifestations followed, including ecstatic laughter, falling on the floor, prostrations, convulsions, loss of bodily control, and visions. There were also some manifestations of animal sounds, including the roaring of lions. Collectively known as 'drunkenness in the Holy Spirit', most of these manifestations had been witnessed in previous revivals, not least during the meetings of the Quakers in Britain. Whilst the media made a great play about the roaring (animal) noises, the fact is that they constituted a very small part of what went on. Inevitably they received a disproportionate amount of attention in both the secular and Christian press, with many in the latter seemingly outraged by such 'out of control' behaviour.

Quickly dubbed 'The Toronto Blessing' (by a respected British religious journalist, Ruth Gledhill), the Christian church was suddenly front page news, not for sexual scandals or the misappropriation of money, but for behaviour that features prominently in the New Testament. Here was, for the TACF (at that time known as TAV), something totally unexpected, though welcome, and something exciting, if somewhat disconcerting.

It's worth pausing at this juncture to ponder the significance of the manifestations. Jonathan Edwards, *Distinguishing Marks of a Work of the Spirit of God* (1741)[10], offers the following cautionary advice

> A work [of the Holy Spirit] is not to be judged by an effect on the bodies of men, such as tears, trembling, groans, loud outcries, agonies of body, or the failing of bodily strength. The influence the minds of the persons are under, is not to be judged one way or the other, whether it be from the Spirit of God or not by such effects on the body. The reason is because the Scripture nowhere gives us any such rule.

He adds a perspective that both opponents and proponents of the Toronto Blessing have tended to ignore: 'We cannot conclude that persons are under the influence of the true Spirit, because we see such effects upon their bodies. Nor on the other hand have we any reason to conclude, from any such outward appearances, that persons are not under the influence of the Spirit of God.' However, a hugely respected figure like Dr Martyn Lloyd-Jones (minister at Westminster Chapel London, England, 1938-68, and later succeeded by Dr R.T. Kendall), has pointed out that it would be surprising if the bodies of men and women were not affected by a powerful demonstration of the Holy Spirit.[11]

An equally respected clergyman, the Reverend J.F.K. (Sandy) Millar, formerly of Holy Trinity Brompton (Anglican) church, made the acute observation that what was needed was wisdom to discern the work of the Spirit – for only the Spirit can rightly discern the operation of the Spirit, not the flesh, adding: 'To attempt to discern the Spirit with the flesh is like an attempt to describe the sunset with algebraic equations – it simply can't be done', and in the same article[12] says that the fruit is the true test of the work of the Spirit. Judged by these criteria, there were many other more substantial features taking place that Thursday evening. These included healings (both physical and emotional), an intense conviction of sin, radical life-changing encounters with God, and a number of conversions. Incidentally, there are almost invariably conversions in the meetings at TACF even though they are ostensibly convened for Christians. For some, the laughter was like the surgery the Holy Spirit was performing on them, bringing up from the past unforgiveness or hurts that had been sublimated because they had been too excruciatingly painful to deal with. That night too, marriages, some in a state of considerable disrepair, were healed and put back on track, with renewed love and commitment.

One thing was absolutely clear from that first night: TACF could never be the same as before, and the congregation and its leaders learned that whenever the Holy Spirit truly moves in power, the unexpected must be expected. That's what took place in the New Testament, why should the present-day church be any different? Of course, some of the congregation found this turn of events threatening, and some left, and though this was regrettable, there was every intention of pursuing the direction laid down by the Holy Spirit. John Arnott was determined that nothing – or nobody – was to deflect or destroy the Spirit's powerful intervention. Indeed the events of January 20th came as a surprise to many men and women, and blew away years of arid Christian belief and behaviour and, more importantly, restored the excitement that they had either long forgotten or never previously experienced.

Clearly the impact of the outpouring on John and Carol Arnott is of primary concern, but it is also helpful to chronicle how the 'blessing' affected other people with whom they worked, and also on Randy Clark himself. So let's begin with him.

Randy Clark

In his autobiography *Lighting Fires* (published by Charisma, 1998), he traces his personal and Christian experience up to and after 1994. Today he has a global ministry and heads up a network of churches called Renewal Ministries International. Prior to 1994, his life had been far from easy, with a great deal of hardship, even poverty, and a broken first marriage. He became a pastor of a decidedly obscure church and worked in a doughnut store to supplement his meagre earnings. He was powerfully impacted by the ministry, personal example and generosity of John Wimber, but was suspicious of prophecy and was reluctant to allow signs and wonders to operate in his own church (by 1994 he was the senior pastor of St Louis Vineyard Fellowship). Before travelling to Toronto he had been given a prophetic word which suggested that God was going to start something really significant in Canada which would have an effect on the whole of North America. Somewhat surprisingly perhaps, this reassurance did not either help with or increase his faith, and his lame response to any encouragement was to 'hope' that God would make his presence felt in a tangible manner.

Randy arrived in Toronto without any idea of what God intended for the four days of meetings, and he was certainly taken aback by the laughter ('wave after wave of great belly laughter filled the auditorium'), and in general he had never witnessed previously anything like it. He did though recognise that something ground-breaking was taking place, was awed by the whole experience and, in addition, knew from his avid study of revival history, that 'the experiences of the early revivalists in church history were coming alive in Toronto as God began to break up the fallow ground of spiritual apathy.' He also understood that God was restoring the excitement to church life, in a manner reminiscent of the first century events in the Acts of the Apostles. A particularly welcome aspect for him was the homecoming of the prodigals (Luke 15), whose return to the Father's house is a magnificent reason for celebration, even a party: 'After all, this is just the first phase of [the] great End-Time outpouring of the Holy Spirit.'

In the early weeks of 1994, Randy also became convinced that 'the event' was not something restricted to Toronto, not something to be confined to merely one part of the North American continent. He saw that one of the dominating themes emanating from Toronto was that of mission, a belief that he shared with John Arnott, who realised that Toronto would be used to ignite other revival fires throughout the world. This understanding on Randy's part was enshrined in a sermon entitled 'Spend and Be Spent', which actually constituted a call to the mission field. This was not a new or novel emphasis because missionary expansion has frequently accompanied revival, as it did following the great revival in eighteenth-century Britain led by John Wesley. This time, however, one of those responding to the sermon was the preacher himself: Randy Clark.

Randy has revisited Toronto on a number of occasions since the first tumultuous seven months of 1994, but he has also had time to reflect on what he calls the 'greatest fruits' of the Toronto Blessing. First, he mentions the revival in Mozambique, where Rolland and Heidi Baker (both impacted dramatically by the Blessing) have planted 6,000 churches and also started a life-saving and life-transforming ministry amongst the children of that strife-torn and desperately poor country[13]. Second, he refers to the number of Muslim people who are being converted. Third he refers to what he calls 'the spreading of the fire around the world', in such countries as

Brazil, China and the Ukraine. This has come about not just because of the ministry of leaders, but also because of ordinary people who have been renewed and refreshed by the Holy Spirit. Weary, often disillusioned, men and women have been reinvigorated and freshly receptive to whatever God intends for them. To these fruits John and Carol Arnott add the whole idea of increased expectation: '[We have] seen an expectation in the hearts of many Christians now that, when they go to church something should happen. There's a greater expectation that the presence of God should be felt and experienced in some way.'

Randy Clark was God's instrument for what John Arnott calls an 'explosive' work of the Holy Spirit: 'The meetings in Toronto [in 1994] were not hyped under his leadership nor fuelled with charismatic enthusiasm. Randy shared his heart with us, and the Holy Spirit came in great power. We could not keep up with the testimonies because they were so numerous'. Randy's equally passionate view is expressed as follows: 'The outpouring was what both John and I for many years had dreamed of and prayed for . . . I thank God that he sent me to Toronto; going was pivotal to my future in ministry.' He was, however, not the only person to feel the considerable impact of the events of January 1994, and there are others whose recollections are equally striking and memorable, including Jeremy and Connie Sinnott.

Jeremy and Connie Sinnott

In the context of how the outpouring affected the staff at what was then the Toronto Airport Vineyard (TAV), the views of Jeremy and his wife Connie are highly relevant. They had both attended the kinship group that met in the living room of John Arnott's mother, and both loved the gentle and reflective manner of Vineyard worship, which incidentally also characterises the songs they have written either together or individually. Jeremy was impressed from the start by John and Carol's willingness to be open and vulnerable – in fact, they were the first pastors to be like this because, after all, pastors are not meant to be vulnerable like other men and women. A misnomer, of course, but one that pervades a very high percentage of churches. 'John Arnott won us over,' say the Sinnotts, 'by being real and won our hearts as a consequence.'

This was a challenging time [1987–88] personally for both Jeremy and Connie. In particular Jeremy found it hard to give up being the principal of a large Christian School, where he felt fulfilled, in order to become an associate pastor with the Toronto Airport Christian Fellowship [TACF]. This was very much a double role involving leadership and pastoral responsibilities. As Jeremy explains, 'We weren't moving in the Holy Spirit very much yet, so it was quite a stretch for us when we met John and Carol. However, our hearts were drawn into a much deeper intimacy with the Lord and we were greatly impacted by John and Carol's walk with the Lord'.

John especially, but also Carol, were instrumental in breathing new life and vigour into the experience of Jeremy and Connie. John did this by emphasising the crucial importance of inner healing and the need to hear God's voice. Listening in this way not only led to intimacy with God, it was also vital before embarking on any course of action. That process of renewal and refreshment for both Jeremy and Connie was given an enormous boost by the events of January 1994, as Jeremy himself explained:[14] 'Having been trained at Grace Theological Seminary, with its stridently conservative and fervently anti-charismatic outlook, my initial response was one of considerable bemusement, with a distinct feeling of uncertainty about what was happening. I wasn't alone in feeling like this, but the months and years that followed clarified the whole issue for me. People were healed (including deaf people) and "power evangelism" [John Wimber's famous phrase] was apparent from day one.'

Jeremy recalls many other facets of the Blessing that have become well known: 'Strong manifestations of the Spirit and intercessory prayers were apparent too, while marriages on the verge of terminal decline were healed. Pastors, many of whom were ready to leave their congregations, went home to re-fire their people with fresh vision and an intimate sense of God's intimacy and love. People at the church too were changed to the extent of being revolutionised by the power of God. "This is the Lord" was an oft-repeated refrain in the early meetings, a sentiment invariably expressed with a mixture of gratitude and incredulity.'

Over ten years on, Jeremy and Connie recall with clarity the 'fresh awareness' of God's love informing the meetings as well, which was, in their view, much more important than the manifestations. There was also for them personally a sense of glorious release taking precedence over the crippling fear of the orthodox – which troubles most people from time to time. What was so encouraging to them, as to John and Carol Arnott, was that the reality of the Holy Spirit was 'felt' in the normal church services, not just at the big conferences, and also all over the world.

So Jeremy and Connie see the Blessing as transferable, the goal being joyful intimacy with the Father, replacing dryness and a deficiency of spiritual energy. Their considered view is that renewal was already in the church, though obviously not to the same degree, before January 1994 unleashed it on the world. Corporately they welcomed the refreshment of the Spirit, although at first they did not know how long it would last. John Arnott frequently warned them 'that it could end tomorrow'. It didn't, of course, and another side-effect for Jeremy and Connie is that their personal ministries took on a new dimension: they have ministered in many parts of the world since 1994. They have continued to work at TACF, happy to follow and submit to the benign and facilitating leadership of John and Carol because, in Jeremy's words, 'the Arnotts you see on stage are the people they are in everyday life. John and Carol are unassuming, non-manipulative people with a "realness" about them that is truly impressive. They constantly insist that people (whoever they are) must not get in the way of what the Spirit is seeking to do. That is the secret of their successful leadership and pastoring of the blessing over the past decade.'[15]

Jeremy and Connie's delight in what happened in 1994 and subsequently has not diminished with the passing years, especially the creative combination of worship, intimacy and power, ideas creatively explored in their book, *A Celebration of One*[16]. They have experienced equally powerful meetings in their travels too. In a meeting in the Philippines, to which people had travelled for many miles, some of them through floods caused by a typhoon, people quickly responded to a call for salvation and for healing. 'We had never previously seen (in meetings led by us) such a high percentage of people who were healed physically,' say the Sinnotts. In another meeting on the island of Mindano, the passionate intensity in worship increased to the point that Jeremy was unable to lead them to a place of quiet intimacy in worship. For more than twenty minutes people wailed and cried out, fully engaged with God: 'The people seemed unaware that we were there,' says Connie. They then realised that God had sent them there to teach men and women how to go deeper into intimacy with the heavenly Father. In fact, all those itinerating out of Toronto declare that intimacy with God is the primary message they are carrying as a result of the Toronto Blessing.

The Sinnotts also point to the huge numbers of conversions since 1994, something they rightly consider to be the 'greatest miracles of all in the Christian faith'. Realistically, they accept that the city of Toronto itself (one of the most ethnically diverse places in the world) has not been impacted in truly life-transforming ways. This is something of a disappointment to them and they pray daily that the Blessing's influence on churches, leaders and congregations will permeate through society as a whole. So there's no sense of settling down, no retreating back to comfort zones, rather an expectation of further robust and life-changing move of the Holy Spirit. In this desire they are at one with John and Carol who are convinced that God is calling his church to seek his face, with fasting and weeping, and to pray unceasingly for revival. There is clear, biblical thinking behind this conviction too, as John wrote in an editorial for the 1997 *Spread the Fire* magazine: 'Amidst the hopelessness and despair that has gripped the nations, an awareness seems to be emerging that God could be the one who has a solution to the trouble and unrest. As Christians, we are certain of it, persuaded that we need a revival – an unprecedented, worldwide outpouring of the Holy Spirit that will turn things around and restore righteousness and godliness to the people. The good news is that God has promised that if we pray, He will restore.'

Jeremy and Connie have been thrilled to observe many healings (physical, mental and emotional) occurring at TACF, of which Carol Berg's healing was truly remarkable. By 1994 she had endured twenty years of ill health, to the point that she was not expected to live much longer. This was so because of serious problems with immune system. She had heard that 'something was happening at TACF.' and so she decided to attend a meeting. She didn't like the meeting, she didn't like the worship either. Thoroughly disappointed, she felt the Spirit directing her to 'Go find Randy Clark'. She was obedient. He prayed for her, and she was given a vision of 'God's Party', to which all men and women of whatever age are invited, and where all can drink. On the floor, she fell asleep, and subsequently needed to be carried to her car. Later she reflected that as a 'dignified, professional woman', this was surprising behaviour indeed. But four days later she realised that her terrible headaches and crippling muscle pain had gone. She had been completely healed. Since that time she has travelled extensively, especially in America, and in Rochester High Security Prison, Minneapolis, she prayed for an old man dying of an incurable heart condition and he was completely healed too: God, quite literally, gave him a new heart. Carol's healing was miraculous; and her story could be replicated many times over.

Jeremy and Connie Sinnott had been associated, in a full-time capacity, with John and Carol Arnott for seventeen years before 1994 whereas Steve Long did not join the staff of TACF until June 1994. Currently Senior Associate Pastor, with overall responsibility for the day-to-day operation of the church in terms of administration, cell groups, counselling etc, plus overseeing the administration of the major conferences such as 'Catch The Fire', he was significantly affected by the events of January 1994.

Steve Long

Steve was, in the early years of the 1990s, an assistant pastor in a Baptist church (Credit Valley Community Church) in Mississauga, a town some seven miles from Toronto. By the end of 1992–93, he found himself increasingly open to the Holy

Spirit, both theologically and experientially; and at this time he kept a journal recording times when God spoke to him directly and unambiguously, and he began to listen more acutely to God's voice. In reality, he was moving away from Credit Valley Community Church and was directed by several Christian acquaintances (including his senior pastor, John Freel) towards the then Toronto Airport Vineyard church. At this time too, he felt a growing, though merely informal, relationship with John and Carol Arnott.

Initially though he was not enthusiastic. In fact, his reaction to what he observed was anything but ordinary and straightforward. His mind characterised the events he witnessed as 'bizarre', indeed his theological training and background convinced him that they were 'shocking'. Against this insistent feeling he placed the fact that he was 'dry spiritually' and was not reading his Bible or praying with any consistency or enjoyment.

Steve's relationship and his links with John and Carol Arnott, were strengthened immeasurably on the Monday following 20 January 1994, when John Arnott said that he (Steve) needed to 'come to carry people out of the meetings'. Sitting in the back row at Dixie Road, Steve encountered the Holy Spirit in a real and life-transforming way. Together with his wife and mother, Steve was about to leave when Randy Clark prayed for them, and this is what occurred: 'I was not looking for it but I met with the Holy Spirit in a dynamic manner, including crumpling unceremoniously to the floor. I didn't mean to do this, but I was suffused with the peace of God in a manner I had not felt for quite some time. Next morning I devoured the Acts of the Apostles: I was now reading a whole different Bible, and enjoying it.'

Life now began to change radically for Steve in several different ways. The following Sunday, John Freel offered Steve to help with the administration at the church, initially for a period of one month only. This arrangement meant that Steve worked with John Arnott and his team during the week but attended Credit Valley Church at the weekend. This arrangement lasted for five months until June 1994 when Steve formally joined the staff at TACF. Now, in addition to sundry administrative tasks, he led three evening meetings each week and, according to him, 'loved it'. Even more significantly perhaps, his own Christian life began to change too, with increased spiritual expectations in a way not previously experienced. But it was not an immediate or quick spiritual 'fix', rather it was something that came as the awakening continued, though it has intensified over the years. Part of this process included working through the pain and anguish of a split in a previous church, plus the need for lots of life's wounds to be healed. The choice he faced, with his wife (Sandra) was stark: either embrace the awakening and go through a process of painful inner healing and forgiveness, or move. They embraced it, and today Steve and Sandra often minister together in different parts of the world, bringing God's love and acceptance to needy men and women.

Steve Long is a calm, balanced, reflective, intelligent man. Theologically trained, with a background in conservative evangelical churches, including a Brethren ancestry, he would totally oppose anything that smacks of the spurious and the sham. Pretence is totally alien to him, and he is only interested in the reality of the Christian life, and in conversation with the author in Toronto he made it pristinely clear that he considers the awakening to be a genuine movement of the Holy Spirit, certainly not something bogus or manipulated. He also has enormous respect, even admiration for John Arnott's qualities as a leader – he identifies him as a visionary[17] (not a dreamer) who is continually looking two or three years ahead. Steve particularly appreciates the fact too that the Arnotts have not changed as people since being catapulted into the fame academy of the Christian world. It is no exaggeration to say that Steve and Sandra are honoured to be chosen to work at TACF under the spiritual guidance and authority of John and Carol. Respect for them also became quickly apparent when Ian Ross kindly spoke to the author about his response to the Toronto awakening.

Ian and Janice Ross

Ian Ross' life experience was totally different to that of Steve Long. He joined the staff at TACF in the summer of 1993, initially part-time, then full time from September that year, after a fulfilling and successful career as a financial analyst with IBM. He had attended his first service at Dixie Road in 1990, loved the Vineyard churches' way of operating, but really knew very little about the ongoing, daily work and influence of the Holy Spirit. Two years earlier, in Nicaragua, he had witnessed at first hand God's transforming power, and saw dynamism in the church in the form of signs and wonders. 'Now,' in Ian's captivating phrase, he 'believed the Book.'

The Toronto Blessing transformed the life and ministry of both Ian and Janice Ross, although initially she in particular did not like what was happening. They wrestled with their roles as leaders at TACF because they had received no formal training, nor did they consider themselves to be church leadership material. They felt totally unqualified. But they had reckoned without the astute leadership insights of John and Carol who nurtured and encouraged them, in a manner reminiscent of a spiritual father and mother.

Sometimes this spiritual guidance and nurturing took the form of what can only be characterised as 'shock therapy'. Invited to join John and Carol in Holland, they discovered, to their consternation that after half a day, John left for Egypt. Ian and Janice now faced the daunting prospect of addressing thirteen meetings before a crowd of between seven hundred and a thousand people. Such a task would have stretched the resources of an experienced leader, but to make matters even worse Ian had only two messages he could use while Janice had never spoken before.

They survived, and Janice in particular was a different person on their return to Toronto. On reflection, it is clear that John and Carol perceived in Ian and Janice those qualities of character and gifting that God could use, especially their realisation of, and devotion to, God as Father, and their love of the intimacy of his presence. Equally the Arnotts must have felt that any risk with Ian and Janice was worth taking. Ian and Janice look back to the awakening in Toronto as a defining moment in their Christian lives. It had a truly dramatic effect on both and led, ultimately, to a ministry that takes them around the world. They had always loved praying for people and they could do this each time they attended a meeting (or led) at TACF. Refreshed and renewed by the powerful infusion of the Holy Spirit, they grew in the depth of their confidence in their heavenly Father, and love to see his power at work transforming the lives of men and women. 'We are,' says Ian, 'addicted to the presence of God. We [constantly] need to press into God, to that intimate place where we feel free to rest our head on the Father's bosom. We can no longer survive with just a theological understanding of his affection for us. We need to experience this for ourselves, to own this truth in our hearts. If anyone truly experiences this blessing, then [it] will change every facet of [their] life. A Divine encounter with God will change everything.'

As with Steve Long, Ian Ross came form a conservative theological (Brethren) background, while his experience in industry had developed and honed in him leadership qualities and skills which – after January 1994 – God could sanctify and use for his purposes. Like Randy Clark, Ian considers the work of Rolland and Heidi Baker in Mozambique to be an important fruit of the awakening in Toronto. 'There,' he says, 'the true foundations of the church are being restored: love based, with what most people see as normal church being accompanied by the heart of God in a truly supernatural way. The work in Mozambique exemplifies what God has always been looking for: lovers.' And Ian is emphatic that one of the great features of Toronto is the way in which John and Carol, in their leadership, model the love of God so transparently. This is the view too of Peter and Heather Jackson, currently associate pastors at TACF, who combine working one week each month at the church with an extensive itinerant ministry throughout the world. Before 1994 they were pastors within the Vineyard grouping of churches as well as being friends of John and Carol Arnott.

Peter and Heather Jackson

Both view the Toronto phenomenon as a 'revival'. 'God,' they say, 'is waking up the church, refreshing it, and preparing for a worldwide harvest. It is the church identifying with people and returning to its first love, together with a sense of ongoing mission.' To them, it's not about church politics or programmes, rather it's about passion for Jesus; a love relationship, in other words, so that people's lives are filled, not with destructively self-centred thoughts, but with the thoughts of God and lives of holiness.

Peter and Heather were, self-confessedly, surprised – even astounded – by the events of January 1994. They first attended on January 21st and then for ten consecutive evenings thereafter. At this time, Heather in particular was a thoroughly disillusioned Christian. She had stopped attending church regularly, probably going only one Sunday in five, and was, in fact, so discouraged that she wanted to leave the Christian ministry altogether. Peter too was equally discouraged and considerably in need of refreshment and revitalising. Both were discouraged by the lack of lasting fruit (Gal. 5:22,23) and the disgruntled attitudes of some of the members in a church plant they were starting in a city outside Toronto' So what happened?

A dynamic experience

When Randy Clark prayed that evening nothing took place. But after John Arnott had prayed for the Holy Spirit to take away past discouragements, Peter wept and then laughed for three hours until he ached physically. Heather also wept, and she comments: 'I felt that God was inviting me to walk with him, it seemed as if the grave clothes were coming off after many weary years of Christian service and ministry. I now knew that God was with me, personally and individually.' She also knew that God was taking off the grave clothes of religion, fear and self-effort. Instead Peter and Heather were experiencing the weight of God's presence, his dynamism and revelatory power. Both are convinced that the Toronto Blessing is not about 'fear of man', or human control, or human manipulation or even intimidation, or self-importance – it's about God 'reviving *his* church in order to fulfil his purposes, not ours.'

In private conversation and also when preaching, Peter and Heather frequently refer to the Toronto phenomenon as a 'revival of nobodies from nowhere'. By this they mean that it's not about big name or glamorous or charismatic speakers blessed with great personal gifts of eloquence[18] and intelligence; instead it's about all people coming into the fullness of the Holy Spirit. In this sense, it is pertinent to say that at TACF the Holy Spirit works as powerfully in the ordinary meetings as he does in the big conferences. It also reaffirms that Jesus is the only 'hero' of the Christian faith, which is a necessary refreshing antidote to the posturing self-importance that so often masquerades for true and genuine Christian commitment these days. The Holy Spirit, after all, is only interested in revealing Jesus, not establishing high-profile ministries. Toronto, in the opinion of Peter and Heather, emphasises that 'we do not need to give God a helping hand'. How true.

Characteristics in common

The individuals referred to above had a number of characteristics in common. They all had considerable experience of church life, with strong evangelical backgrounds and, in some cases, of the Vineyard churches then presided over internationally by John Wimber, for whom they had enormous respect. Worship and prayer were immensely important to them, but they longed for more direct and immediate experience of the Holy Spirit. They also used words such as 'dry' and 'disillusioned', even 'apathy', to identify their spiritual condition prior to the events of January 1994.

Guy Chevreau and Curtis Hinds

Two other men who fitted into the 'dry' category were Dr Guy Chevreau and Curtis Hinds. The former was a self-confessed 'burned out' Baptist pastor when the Toronto outpouring began. Within days he began to receive the Blessing himself, since which time his ministry has taken him all over the world. He says: 'Personally I have never known such a sense of fruitfulness and fulfilment. It feels like I'm doing what the Lord has prepared me to do all my adult life.' Curtis Hinds, an itinerant evangelist prior to coming to TACF in 1992, was similarly burned out and also confused. As he says himself, 'I was so works orientated that it was hard for me to just draw near to God for no other reason than to draw near.' In the prayerful atmosphere of God's presence, however, his heart was healed, leading to a more intimate relationship with his heavenly Father. Curtis is frequently asked, 'What's next?' to which he responds: 'What else is there?' He says this because he is enjoying the Father's Blessing so much that he describes himself as a 'soldier with a party hat on'. He also points to the fact that he saw more conversions in the four years following 1994 than in the previous ten years. Significantly, he has broadened the range of his ministry by establishing orphanages for Brazil's huge number of street children. His call to that country came in a vision he had after the outpouring began in which he saw multitudes of children all wearing the face of his own son. He was moved by this vision that he now spends a great deal of his time in Brazil.

Incredulity and amazement

These testimonies reflected above are distinctly encouraging, but they cannot disguise the fact that the events of January 1994 were surprising. Jeremy Sinnott, for example, told the *Sunday Telegraph* that he didn't know why God had picked their little church, a sentiment shared by many in the church. (Recently in conversation with Jeremy the author expressed amazement that he still attends at least four evening meetings each week, to which he replied: 'I love it – just seeing God at work in people's lives is one of the most thrilling, indeed exhilarating, experiences in the world.') The TACF church embraced what was happening, however, being convinced from the outset that God was at work, and soon visitors from as far away as Australia, Britain and Japan came flocking to what one Canadian described critically, though accurately, as 'an unimpressive location at a nondescript, flat industrial plaza'; and soon it grew to a thousand people a night, necessitating the renting of a banquet hall to accommodate the burgeoning crowds. On the North American continent, congregations in Chicago, San Francisco, Houston, Dallas, Orlando and Lakeland, Florida, reported experiencing similar events to those in Toronto.

The sheer ordinariness too of the setting surprised many visitors, as did the intensity of the worship, the excitement, the extent of the manifestations, and the large number of conversions. Perhaps the two words that most appropriately described how the men and women featured here felt are 'incredulity' and 'amazement': incredulity at the power of the Spirit's work, and amazement that God should have chosen an ordinary church, in an ordinary building, and certainly ordinary leaders. On the other hand, the history of revival shows that certain places are, for whatever reason, particularly anointed, and in this context it's worth mentioning the fact that George Jeffreys[19] (died 1962), the twentieth-century British evangelist and founder of the Elim Pentecostal movement, had conducted renewal meetings in Toronto as far back as 1924, when scenes similar to those in 1994 were witnessed. But what about the reactions of John and Carol Arnott who, by 1994, had been leading churches in the Toronto area since 1981?

And so to the Arnotts

John and Carol shared Peter and Heather Jackson's astonishment at the unexpected turn of events. As John says in *Experience The Blessing* (Renew Books, 2000): 'We were overwhelmingly surprised when many Christian leaders from around the world came thirsting for a more intimate relationship with God. For our part, we have only tried to stay simple and humble and keep out of the Holy Spirit's way, as even now He continues to move in power upon the hungry.' He also says that 'our hearts have been thrilled by so many miraculous testimonies. We have watched in amazement as the fire of God has become a worldwide phenomenon, touching virtually every nation.' He is straightforwardly honest and uncomplicated in his later admission: 'It never occurred to us that God would throw a massive party where people would laugh, roll, cry and become so empowered that their emotional hurts were just lifted off them.' Time and again in their preaching John and Carol use the appellation 'party' when referring to the story of the Prodigal's return in Luke 15, to express their immense delight in what happened in January 1994 and since. There is an important additional dimension too: they have repeatedly said that they felt 'the least qualified' to lead a movement with a global impact.

Unexpected the events certainly were; and vastly different from the 'subdued and comfortable level' (their description) they had been accustomed to in their church lives. Since April 1984, however, they had treasured a prophetic word from Mike Bickle, senior pastor of Metro Christian Fellowship in Kansas City, Missouri. With his pastoral staff he had been meditating on the story in Genesis 40, which chronicles Pharaoh's actions in throwing his cupbearer and baker into prison. Subsequently the baker is beheaded, but the cupbearer is restored to his place of service. After much prayer, Bickle felt that God was saying this: 'The Church will undergo ten years of restraint, like being in a dungeon. The two men represent two ministries. The Lord will deal with those ministries that, like the baker, sow the bread of the Word with hypocrisy, thus producing pride and arrogance. Then, after ten years, those ministries that sowed the Word of God with humility, which produced good spiritual fruit, will emerge from the prison and serve new wine to the King.'

Even earlier in 1975, Dr David Yonggi Cho, of Seoul, Korea, had said: 'When I came to Canada, the Holy Spirit spoke in my heart, "Son, you have come to the place which I chose. This country is the country I chose to fill the gap".' Then, in 1985, Bickle and his leadership team heard this word from God: 'When you see the Mississippi River flood and even change its direction, that will be a sign that a mighty move of the Spirit is about to come.'[20] Later, in 1993, many floods in the American mid-west occurred, causing the Mississippi River to change its direction at different places; and that same year John and Carol began to pray for a fresh anointing from God. In November

1993, after a visit to Argentina, they returned to Toronto determined to 'believe God for more'. The word 'more' could certainly be used to describe their church life in January 1994. The first month or so flew by, with the meetings, according to Randy Clark, growing in intensity all the time. At this point it is alleged that someone in the church suggested to John Arnott that they had had a great time, but perhaps it should all be 'cut back and geared down a bit', to which John apparently replied: 'You can cut back if you wish, I'm not, because this is what I have been waiting for all my Christian life.'

Clearly John and Carol were thrilled by the events of 1994: 'I had never seen the likes of it in all my thirty-eight years of being a Christian. This was my church. We were not among strangers or in a meeting where we knew only a few. I knew that my church would not "put this on". God had come powerfully among us. With all of our praying about revival, I never stopped to think what it might look like.' John and Carol had always been humble and vulnerable in their ministry, and they are convinced that those core values were present in Randy Clark too, which is why, in their opinion, God chose him to trigger the Toronto outpouring. An amusing anecdote relates to an acquaintance of Clark's, who when told about the events in Toronto said, 'It can't be the Randy Clark I know.' But it was.

Overwhelmed they may have been, but from the start John and Carol were convinced that such happenings could not – nor were intended to be – confined or restricted to Toronto. This was an event with much wider connotations and much wider application too. It became quickly apparent that there would be a two-way movement: people associated with TACF, or who had been impacted there, would take the 'good news' to other parts of the world, while visitors also came to Toronto from many, many nations, eager to experience for themselves God's refreshing and reinvigorating love. With this influx of people, plus their own international travelling, plus the additional tasks now thrust upon them in terms of pastoral care and administration, John and Carol's lives could never be the same again, nor could there be any return to the less frenetic lifestyle they had enjoyed previously. As an example of this change, they travelled to minister in Hungary in February

1994, where phenomenon akin to that in Toronto occurred. The Blessing was spreading with amazing speed, as was the attention paid to it in the secular and religious press.

Widening Circles: Pittsburg, USA

Bill and Melinda Fish visited Toronto for the first time in November 1994. After many years of pastoral ministry they were discouraged and emotionally numb. More fundamentally, they feared that they had 'somehow missed God'. The strategies that apparently worked for other people did not seem to work in their church, at least not with any consistency, and almost never for any length of time. Each approach – whether it be prayer, fasting, evangelism or growth seminars – would end on a note of anti-climax. In reality, they longed for true and lasting revival, which never happened for them.

But there, in Toronto, they felt the first powerful infusion of God into their lives for many years and, significantly, 'felt completely surrounded by a sense of the love of God'. And within weeks of returning home to their church in Pittsburg, their church was transformed. Laughter broke out in their meetings, five healings took place, all verified medically; and since then the Holy Spirit has showed up at every single service 'in a new dimension of his powerful presence'. Men and women hungry for God have come to Pittsburg from south-western Pennsylvania, West Virginia and Ohio, and gone away with renewed love and passion for Jesus. The testimony of Bill and Melinda indicates unequivocally that the Toronto Blessing is transferable, with the Holy Spirit demonstrating himself in clear, unambiguous terms, the consequences being changed lives, re-fired passion for Jesus, and a new sense of excitement in church.

Widening Circles: Sydney, Australia

Adrian Gray, an experienced pastor of the Christian Life Centre, Annan, Sydney, says that the events at TACF were a touchpaper, rekindling the flames of revival that had always existed in his heart but which had begun to go out. He attended the last meeting held in the old Dixie Road building, and, after responding to Jeremy Sinnott's invitation to come forward for prayer, found himself deeply affected, impacted by the Holy Spirit and returned home to Australia doubly determined to pursue revival, personally and collectively in his church. Since 1994, a minimum of five services have been held each week, with an increasing intensity of the power and presence of God.

The above accounts are but two representatives of thousands of others from all across the world that could be cited. Bill, Melinda and Adrian were insistent on finding God for themselves, but then were equally intent on 'walking in God's love and giving it away'.

Widening Circles: England

After Canada and America, more visitors flocked to Toronto from Britain than other country in the world. The momentous impact on Britain began to be apparent in May 1994, more particularly May 24th and May 29th. This was largely due, in the first instance, to the influence and preaching of Elli Mumford, who addressed a meeting of English leaders, including Nicky Gumbel of Holy Trinity Brompton, at her home. After recounting what had happened to her in Toronto, she prayed for the leaders (from all of the major denominations) and Toronto-like manifestations erupted dramatically. This was on May 24th.

Five days later the Blessing (which John and Carol from the very start referred to refer to as 'The Father's Blessing') was experienced by large congregations at the evening services at Holy Trinity Brompton. This meeting was again addressed by Elli Mumford, wife of John Mumford, the Vineyard leader in south London. The Holy Spirit was powerfully present on both occasions, and Elli later reflected that she had never experienced such love and joy, expressing the view that the 'best parties' are to be found in God's house. That same evening, albeit at a different venue (Rob Warner's church,

Herne Hill Baptist Church), personal ministry continued past 2 p.m., an unusual though welcome occurrence. During the following week Toronto-like phenomenon were witnessed at Kensington Temple, though Colin Dye, the senior pastor, and his leadership team eventually decided not to go down the revival centre route, opting instead to focus on Christ, not the phenomena, and evangelism, not experience. This choice must not be construed as meaning disenchantment or disaffection on the part of Kensington Temple, as Colin himself explains: 'The effect of the Toronto awakening was to refresh and to empower our church, and I regard what happened as an utterly positive event.' He also quotes approvingly Mike Bickle's opinion that 'God offends the mind to reveal the heart.'

But it wasn't only London where the impact of Toronto was observed, as the details relating to four other centres are chronicled here.

Aldershot

Aldershot is widely known as 'the home of the British Army', with a diverse, cosmopolitan population, and includes churches of all the major denominations. At the King's Church (now known as KC21) a 'season of glorious disorder' (C.H Spurgeon's eloquent phrase, quoted in *God's Harvest* by I.D.E. Thomas[21].) ensued, and this is what happened on Sunday, 19 June 1994, five months after the initial outbreak in Toronto: 'It was evident that the Holy Spirit was powerfully at work . . . and people were slain in the Spirit, and the meeting continued until almost 2 a.m. on Monday morning.'[22] For the next three weeks the church met every evening except Saturdays, and subsequently three times weekly, with no apparent let-up in the momentum. The phenomena witnessed at the King's Church included falling down as though dead, laughter and joy, trembling and groaning in the Spirit. In addition, a number of people were quite literally 'frozen' and unable to move. One woman in her late forties said rather bemusedly, 'I was blessed by the Spirit without even asking.' Others were so 'drunk' in the Spirit that they were unable to walk, while others were so overwhelmed by the Spirit's revelations that they wept uncontrollably for long periods. The unusual manifestations transcended age barriers, with young and old alike feeling the power and dynamism of the Holy Spirit. Reflecting on these events ten years on, the senior pastor, Derek Brown, considers what occurred in Aldershot to have been 'an authentic visitation from God, and a powerful demonstration of the Holy Spirit. The lessons we learned then are still being applied today.' Derek also views the Toronto Blessing as a 'definite prophetic statement to the world of what God wants to do in terms of identity, Father God, and the presence of the Holy Spirit.' Similar events were observed too at Ken Gott's church in Sunderland.

Sunderland

This bustling formerly industrial city had seen a profound move of the Holy Spirit at the start of the twentieth-century, and so has a rich spiritual heritage, having witnessed the ministry of the Reverend Alexander Boddy. Sunderland had also been a crucial place in the rise and development of Pentecostalism. By 1994, for a variety of personal, social and religious reasons, Sunderland was again in need – some would say desperate need – of a fresh visitation from God.

One day in August that year Ken Gott describes what he calls 'A Mount Sinai experience': 'James Senior, our youth pastor, who had visited Toronto with us, broke down and wept before the people. Amidst all the laughing, shaking, jerking and carpet time in Toronto, God had shown us that in our ignorance we had not given him his church. We ourselves had held it very tightly and selfishly with all ministry flowing from us and all roads leading to us. We needed to step back, repent, let God be the focus and allow ministry to be released to the whole body of Christ'[23]. After much repentance and weeping, there followed what Ken Gott calls 'a massive outpouring of the Spirit'. This outpouring continued (with the exception of Monday evenings, when there was no meeting) unabated for two and a half years, demonstrating, in Ken Gott's words, 'that although we are ordinary people, we have the most extraordinary God'. This emphasis is surely one of the primary aspects of the Toronto Blessing, the understanding being that even the most exalted preacher or leader must take second place to Jesus in any presentation of the Christian faith. Ken and Lois Gott also explain the thinking behind the Sunderland renewal was based on the Toronto model: 'Since we [were] not pursuing primarily the manifestations but the fruit of changed hearts and lives, we gave time every evening for people to share what God had done in their lives'[24].

Wales

Wales has been appropriately described as the 'Land of Revivals', the most important of which occurred in 1904–05, when for a period of just over a year God's work, to adapt Dr Eifion Evans' famous and eloquent phrase, 'carried all before it, purifying, kindling, spreading, and transforming everything in its path'[25]. For a hundred years, that revival has been a prototype for all other revivals, and on the ninety-fourth anniversary of the beginning of the 1904–05 revival a ministry team led by Wesley and Stacey Campbell arrived in Wales. A meeting in Bangor, North Wales, drew people from a fifty mile radius. Wesley and Stacey spoke on 'The End Time Revival' and 'The Great Harvest', and exhorted those present to give serious consideration to end-time realities.

The meetings were charged with the presence of the Holy Spirit, with many people falling to the ground under the Spirit's power as prophetic words were spoken over them. University students were especially affected, and they left the meeting with renewed zeal for reaching non-Christians. Trevor Baker, of Dudley, England, expressed this forthright opinion: 'I believe that revival could have broken in at this point affecting the lost and the social fabric of the community.'[26] In another meeting, there was wailing, groaning and shouting as men and women met powerfully with God, and at one stage the whole congregation rushed forward, reaching out to God for a fresh visitation of his Spirit. The meeting continued until midnight. At a subsequent meeting in Brecon, Mid Wales, although the congregation was smaller, God's presence was tangible and powerful. Perhaps most powerful of all was the meeting at Moriah Chapel, which witnessed many of the great meetings in 1904–05. The chapel was crammed full, and when Kevin Prosch's song, 'Praise, Praise' was sung, according to one observer, 'it seemed as if there was an angelic chorus aiding the worship; and the chapel was pulsating with life and the tangible Presence of God.'[27] The response to the preaching of the word of God was equally remarkable, with everyone present standing to their feet and crying out to God in prayers of repentance and expectation. The inescapable impression from these meetings was of the re-digging of wells that opened in past revivals.

Spain

In 1998 also, Dr Guy Chevreau led an international ministry team to revisit Betel (Spanish for House of God) Ministries in Spain. Founded by Elliott and Mary Tepper, American missionaries, it cared primarily for recovering heroin addicts, though it grew to care for reformed drug addicts in general, and prostitutes. At a special meeting for Betel leaders in Malaga, Guy Chevreau reported (in *Spread the Fire* for February 1999) as follows: 'There was such a tangible sense of the glory of God [that] it felt like the most significant ten days of our lives.' Elliott Tepper reported that the Holy Spirit 'moved powerfully through the team as they ministered the heart of the Toronto Revival, the Father's love and His awesome grace and forgiveness.'[28] There were dramatic physical and emotional healings too. One man testified that, for the first time in his life, he was able to forgive his father for murdering his mother when he was only two years old. He said too that he was able to forgive himself for ruining his own life in reaction to his dysfunctional upbringing and his life on the streets as a drug addict.

These accounts are instructive and helpful, showing as they do, that manifestations are not the primary aspect of a deep and authentic move of God. A deeper love for Jesus, a desire to share that love with others, conviction of and repentance for sinful behaviour, an increasing devotion to prayer and the word of God are much, much more significant, as is the willingness to obey the guidance of the Holy Spirit. And these are precisely the features of Christina living that John and Carol Arnott emphasised in their many international travels in the immediate aftermath of January 1994. It is perhaps worth listing what Jonathan Edwards considered to be the five main positive fruits to be looked for in any spiritual experience: an honouring of the Lord Jesus, a detachment from selfish pleasure or gain, a hunger for the Scriptures, a concentration on truth, and a deepening of mutual love. The link with the great Jonathan Edwards is made not as an exaggerated claim, but merely to show, in the form of a gentle observation that what took place in Toronto originally, and replicated throughout the world, also had to do with Christian character, Christian reformation and devotion to Jesus, and not just the external phenomena. 'Revival, above everything else,' said the late Dr Martyn Lloyd-Jones, 'is a glorification of the Lord Jesus, the Son of God. It is the restoration of him to the centre of the life of the Church'[29]. This is an important cautionary note when thinking of the Toronto Blessing.

It is also worth pondering, albeit in a general sense, what Dr Martyn Lloyd-Jones also said about periods of renewal and revival: 'Why should the Devil suddenly start doing this kind of thing [referring to the manifestations]. Here is the church in a period of dryness and drought; why should the Devil suddenly do something which draws attention to religion and Jesus Christ? If this is the work of the Devil, well then, the Devil is an unutterable fool'[30].

1994–95 The Spread of the Toronto Blessing and its Detractors

The rise of the Toronto Blessing, as has already been established, was utterly dramatic. John and Carol were quite simply delighted by the Spirit's descent in their strikingly ordinary and, at that time, unthreatening church. Their wholehearted acceptance of what God was doing was followed by its rapid spread into many countries in the world, and particularly in Britain where, according to the statistics, between three and four thousand churches had embraced it by the end of 1994.

That it was controversial cannot be denied, with many opponents lining up to oppose the views and testimonies of those who accepted it. It created a ferment, especially in the evangelical world which, in the case of Britain, the like of which had not been seen since Dr Martyn Lloyd-Jones and John Stott locked horns in 1966 over the hotly-debated question of what constituted true evangelical allegiance. In 1994, as in 1966, opinions rapidly became polarised, and not always to constructive effect, still less to rational debate.

Some commentators viewed it as simply a craze which would soon decline and disappear, while others saw it as a mixed blessing at best. For some, the question was not whether the Toronto Blessing was something God was doing, nor whether it was changing people's lives for the better, but whether it was consistent with the Bible's teaching on the nature of God's blessing in general and the work of the Holy Spirit in particular. One Christian leader (Alan Morrison) denounced it robustly as 'childish and hysterical mimicry'[31], which would seem to be far from a balanced and objective response. More benignly Mark Cartledge identified the main lesson as being the fact that God is concerned with the whole person . . . the challenge being that we all need to become uncomfortable for 'the sake of the Gospel'[32]. To Dr Patrick Dixon, 'one lasting effect of the [Toronto Blessing] has been that tens of millions of believers around the world have shifted one step further towards a combination of Word and Spirit, a synthesis based on sound doctrine and spirituality'[33]. To Dr Margaret Poloma, the academic sociologist, 'Toronto was, at least in part, about learning to find rest for one's soul in God.'[34] In contrast, the Dean of Worcester saw it as 'an expression of hysteria which could lead to a ghetto mentality, and the undermining of an intellectually respectable expression of faith'[35].

During 1994-95 John and Carol were aware of the distinctly contrasting reactions to the movement they were leading, although the accusation most frequently levelled against their church and their leadership was that the Toronto Blessing – and its associated phenomena – was neither 'decent nor in order'.

The crux of this criticism obviously revolves around the definition of what constitutes decency and order. John and Carol frequently teach on four false assumptions about God and his ways of speaking to people.

False Assumption 1: 'I have to understand it or it is not God.' John argues, quite reasonably, in *Keep The Fire* (published by Marshall Pickering in 1995), that God does things at times that are hard to understand and evaluate, which would include some of the phenomena witnessed since January 1994, although most of them have been present in revival throughout the centuries. The biblical evidence too is that when God moves powerfully unusual, even strange, things happen. In this category John would place God's command to Abraham to sacrifice his son Isaac (Gen. 22), and also our Lord's spreading mud on the blind man's eyes before miraculously healing him (Jn. 9).

False Assumption 2: 'The Holy Spirit will never do anything against my will.' At times, as the Bible makes clear, the Holy Spirit overrules a person's will, as he did in the case of Ananias and Sapphira (Acts 5) when his actions brought fear in the wake of the definitive judgement enacted on these two people because they lied to the Holy Spirit.

False Assumption 3: 'It it is truly God I will not be afraid.' John counters this false assumption by saying that people are afraid when God demonstrates himself, not least because we are not accustomed to God revealing himself in enormous, even awesome power.

False Assumption 4: 'God is tidy and proper.' The Bible shows convincingly that the opposite is often the case, in which category John places the story of the man (Lk. 8) afflicted with demonic possession. This was a noisy and extremely complex affair, the very antithesis of tidiness, control and pristine order. The undeniable truth is that the simple, 'humble yet powerful ways of the Holy Spirit offend us, then we will find some logical reason to tidy it up – and pretty soon we find we will not have to worry about His ways bothering us any more. I'd rather have the Holy Spirit come on His terms than mine; even if I am uncomfortable and do not understand.' (John Arnott, *Keep the Fire*, p. 82.)

The latter statement gets to the heart of John and Carol's ministry: their openness to the direction and influence of the Holy Spirit, something which has characterised their preaching and pastoral work since the beginning. Inevitably some critics have construed their approach as sanctioning all sorts of weird and uncontrollable behaviour, but this is not the essence of their teaching at all. John Arnott admitted in an interview with *Charisma* magazine's Gerhard Bially that negative by-products (or tares) often accompanied revival movements, but he later went to say, in the same interview, that he had learned that to uproot tares can sometimes kill the positive results as well, adding that he would rather contend with some fleshly zeal than he would with carnal resistance. Put another way, he would rather have a move of God with defects than no move at all.

The Arnotts' have absolute confidence in the Holy Spirit's ability to control and oversee His sovereign work. It is also a submissive attitude to the overall guidance of the Spirit, although it has to be admitted that such an approach takes men and women completely out of their comfort zones, leaving them vulnerable as a consequence. When this happens, of course, the tendency is to retreat back to the familiar and the well known. However, it must also be accepted that fleshly zeal, in Mike Fearon's careful phrase, can conceal 'serious spiritual overtones within it'.

Facing criticism is never easy. In the immediate aftermath of January 1994, and almost incessantly for the next two years, the Toronto Blessing and its leaders were subjected to a veritable barrage of comment, analysis, theological and sociological critiques, and, in some instances, vituperative criticism. Some of those who embraced the movement accused those who took an opposing view of 'blaspheming against the Holy Spirit'; though, on the other hand, some who were fervently anti the movement characterised the Toronto Blessing as 'demonic'. The use of calumny or pejorative language is never an appropriate or balanced approach, and a most helpful example of evaluative criticism is the charismatic critique entitled *The Mark of the Spirit?*, published by the Paternoster Press in 1998.

John and Carol were not oblivious to the torrent of material appearing in the press and the media, though the time constraints upon them precluded close acquaintance with it: they simply got on with the vision that God had given them. Such attention did not unduly perturb or disturb them, but an event occurred in December 1995 that caused both of them considerable personal pain and even anguish. This was the decision of the Vineyard movement that they could no longer endorse the then Toronto Airport Vineyard and its ministry. That the decision was communicated to them by John Wimber was doubly distressing and saddening for them, not least because they held Wimber in such high esteem; and still do.

5 December 1995: 'You're out'

This was another dramatic, some would say equally tumultuous, day in the life of the then Toronto Airport Vineyard church. At a meeting lasting a considerable length of time, the unequivocal message to John Arnott, and all his senior staff, from John Wimber (accompanied by several other Vineyard Board members) was brusque to the point of brutality: 'You're out.' By this Wimber meant that the relationship between TAV and the rest of the Vineyard movement was decisively at an end. Unsurprisingly, John Arnott was shocked by the Vineyard's non-negotiable stance, and Jeremy Sinnott 'felt fatherless', but the decision was nevertheless accepted. In reality, there was little else that could have been done in the face of an unequivocal decision.

Eight days later, the United Kingdom Association of Vineyard Churches expressed its agreement with the original decision. There were two reasons for this: first an objection to the 'unusual phenomena' witnessed in the Toronto church; and second the apparent refusal of the Toronto leadership to 'minister within the framework and values of the [Vineyard] association'.

A hint regarding Wimber's decision is enshrined in a comment he had made in the English *Church Times* on 30 September 1994. Referring to the occurrence of 'animal' noises, he said that he didn't see it as something that should be affirmed or endorsed by the church and that it should be ignored. An even stronger hint possibly had been published on the Vineyard network, stating that Wimber had endorsed the Blessing with some reserve. His reserve, it is apparent from the same network, related to issues of personal prophecy, making animal sounds in worship, which he perceived as 'weaknesses' in the Toronto Blessing. So serious doubts about the whole Toronto model, it would seem, had led to the decision communicated to Arnott and his leaders on December 5th.

The TAV response was to apologise on 13 December 1995, for any misreading of the Vineyard's concerns (the apology was accepted), but now that they were released from the Vineyard Association, they could pursue the ministry that God had called them to. John Wimber's response, that same day, recognised that God had called the Toronto church 'to a tributary' different from the Vineyard's. Amicability had broken out, but the rumblings continued for many months, especially in the Christian press.

This was swiftly followed on 20 January 1996 (incidentally the second anniversary of the outpouring) by the renaming of the TAV as the Toronto Airport Christian Fellowship (TACF).

Some commentators took the opportunity to put a 'political' spin on Wimber's decision, suggesting that either he was simply 'safeguarding' his own position should the Toronto movement come to grief or was acting in a spirit of competitiveness. Others perceived his decision as an act of authoritarian audacity. Whether any of these motives should appropriately be attributed to him is not entirely easy to determine. There were those who took a different line, declaring that the departure from Vineyard called into question the whole nature and validity of the Toronto movement, the assumption being (wrongly in the author's view) that a large number of people went to Toronto precisely because of its link with John Wimber. A more judicious response would be to see the decision reached on 5 December 1995 as calling into question the whole nature of the relationship between Toronto and the Vineyard Association.

One other interpretation, that of David Hilborn, must be alluded to. He says

> Although personal hurts were later addressed, and although the Toronto church continues to this day as an independent proponent of the Blessing, this very public and somewhat messy divorce effectively put paid to it as a major international movement. If the Blessing has continued as a force within global renewal at all, it has done so inasmuch as it has transmuted into other initiatives – not least Holy Trinity Brompton's Alpha course, which appears to have gained considerable impetus from the Toronto outpouring[36].

Hilborn's opinions are always worth taking seriously, but his perceptions [regarding the end of the Blessing as an international force are not shared by the many associate pastors who journey ceaselessly throughout the world to this day, nor by the many thousands of people who still travel to Toronto for renewal and re-equipping. As *Joy* magazine (published by the Assemblies of God) reported on the 'Catch The Fire' conference for 2003: 'The Toronto Blessing blazes on'.

With reference to the celebrated and hugely successful Alpha courses, the author consulted the vicar of Holy Trinity Brompton, the Reverend J.A.K. (Sandy) Millar, who said this

> The ministry of the Holy Spirit is and always has been absolutely key to Alpha. That said, both Nicky Gumbel and I feel that there was no real connection between the Alpha course and the Toronto Blessing. The basis of the present Alpha course began in 1977, the weekend of the Holy Spirit was introduced in 1982, Nicky Gumbel's *Questions of Life* – which remains the syllabus for the Alpha course today – was published in February 1993, and our first-ever Alpha conference was held here in May 1993.

Millar's careful explanation is extremely valuable, and he concludes like this

> When the movement of the Holy Spirit associated with Toronto began in the spring of 1994, our feeling is that the Alpha course had already been established and running at HTB for many years, and was also beginning to be used by other churches around the UK.

But how did the expulsion from the Vineyard association affect John and Carol Arnott and their fellow leaders? To John Arnott, John Wimber was a dominating figure, a formative influence on his biblical thinking, especially in terms of spiritual gifts, and so he was deeply saddened by the parting. Randy Clark confesses to have been personal grieved by the whole matter: 'grieved by the decision of the Vineyard's leadership, grieved at the reasons given for the decision, grieved by the way the entire matter had been handled, grieved over the ramifications of the decision on the renewal as it continued in Toronto and elsewhere, and grieved over the ramifications of the decision upon the Association of Vineyard Churches.'[37]

John Arnott's equilibrium was not destroyed, however, though Carol says that she was personally devastated by the parting of the ways. He was, though, determined to keep going: a steely resolve accompanied by humility and prayerfulness. He did though feel that, in the 5 December 1995 meeting, they had been disciplined without a precise delineation of the reasons, though of course they were highlighted subsequently. Steve Long was also present at that meeting, and he offers the following impressions

> I was baffled by the process that was being enacted before my eyes. John Arnott, who behaved with calmness and grace throughout the meeting, had sensed in the Spirit a week earlier that there was something amiss in the relationship with the Vineyard association. John Wimber appeared to be tired, but was quite definite and clear in asking John Arnott: 'Am I your pastor or not?' Its implication, as far as I understood this direct question, was that Arnott was not following the Vineyard party line and that

only expulsion would rectify the situation. Clearly this was as difficult a meeting for Wimber as it was for Arnott, and my personal perception is that John Wimber was broken-hearted by the split, but gave his blessing to the Toronto church and its leaders for the future. Despite the turmoil, I felt that God was in the decisions reached that day.[38]

The upshot was that the TACF was able to go in the direction they wished to pursue while, at the same time, allowing the Vineyard association to follow its chosen model for church planting, renewal and church growth.

A brief comment

So by January 1996, John and Carol Arnott were leaders of a church with a new name, with a united leadership, and with a renewed zeal and vigour for God's work and for its spread and developments throughout the world. What a transformation for two people who only ten years earlier had doubted their spiritual and leadership qualities, viewing themselves as being the least qualified people to lead a movement that would eventually have a worldwide impact.

The indisputable fact is, however, that as revivals don't just happen, leaders of renewal or revival don't just happen either. There is a fundamental process of shaping and honing in the lives of men and women who eventually lead significant movements. There is a necessary preparation for ministry, in terms of character, life events and important influences, and it is to this multi-faceted shaping in the lives of John and Carol Arnott that we turn in the next chapter.

Chapter Three

The Shaping

The concept of shaping individuals in preparation for a significant work of God is vitally important. As Evan Roberts said in 1906, 'I am a sinner saved by grace. All the glory must be Christ's. We are nothing, but He can use us. He is waiting for instruments.'[39] That is, God is waiting for 'the human faces', if you wish, who will carry out his work and fulfil his purposes. Thus before coming directly to the personal lives and experiences of John and Carol Arnott, it is important to give a conceptual background to the whole idea of the shaping of men and women in God's service.

What sort of men and women does God choose to be leaders?

The process is one in which his choice, his sovereignty, is as powerfully operative as the choosing of the time and place to reveal himself in dynamic power. When the question is asked, why Ulster in 1859–60, or Wales in 1904–05, or the Hebrides 1949–52?, the response unequivocally is God's sovereignty. Equally when the question is asked why Howell Harris in eighteenth-century Wales, why Zinzendorf in Saxony, why David Brainerd among the Indians, why James McQuilkin in Ireland, or why Duncan Campbell in the Hebrides?, the instant answer once again is God's choice, God's sovereignty. They are men and women who, in Brian Edwards' captivating phrase, 'have eternity in their hearts'.[40] It's as simple and as decisive as that.

Significant leaders of revival are chosen by God: they are his instruments. This is why, for example, Evan Roberts was the designated instrument for the Welsh Revival 1904–05 whereas Dr Peter Price, a well-known contemporary preacher, more gifted naturally, more talented, more robust as a personality, and more intellectually capable, was not. Price vociferously claimed that 'his' revival in Dowlais, South Wales, merited greater attention than the movement led by a man he dismissed as a 'nonentity' and a deluded one at that, but it made no difference. Evan Roberts was chosen, at a momentous time in history, to lead a movement that had huge international ramifications and which, to this day, is viewed as 'the' prototype for revival. Clearly Roberts understood this key principle because reflecting on the revival in 1928–29, he said: 'Any and every revival begins with God. Therefore it is He who must and He who does burden the saints with prayer, choosing the special instruments who are to operate as means of blessing.'

To illustrate this idea in a little more detail, reference will be made to two sources, one biblical, the second the modern corpus of material available on revival.

Biblical Illustration

The example of David in the Old Testament (1 Samuel 17) shows how a significant leader is prepared and chosen for a particular task, his shaping. Briefly attention may be drawn to the following points:

● It was a time of crisis for the Israelites. They faced a deadly enemy, the Philistines, and the whole nation was terrified and dismayed. The outlook was indeed a bleak one unless a hero could be found who would engage in stalwart battle and resistance against the Philistines.

- At that time David was working in the fields owned by his father. This was quite literally hard physical work.
- At first glance he was an unlikely hero; young and not particularly valued or esteemed by his brothers.
- He felt keenly, however, that the Philistines and their aggressive behaviour constituted an offence to the Living God whom David served.
- He encountered jealous opposition from his brothers, his own family.
- David was not, however, put off; he persisted and was utterly determined.
- He was not overwhelmed by Goliath and his intimidating strength. David was full of courage because he knew that God was with him and also with the nation of Israel.
- Significantly he had proved God's power and deliverance in the past, and this gave him enormous confidence. All this was part of the godly shaping of his life. Quite simply, he was strong in the power of the Lord.
- David rejected Saul's armour, the implication being that he could only go in the armour and methods he had proved and tested for himself. Other people's faith and anointing could not work for him. This is a cardinal lesson for us all.
- He went in the Name of the Lord, and in his authority and power. He realised that his power came solely from God; and that the battle was the Lord's, not his.

Three conclusions may be drawn from the example of David. First, he had the heart of a servant, it would seem, from a young age. Second, he had been prepared for the great work of his life, initially, by working at what was a menial and unglamorous task. Significant heroes in God's kingdom don't generally start at the top in the full glare of publicity and success. They start at a much lower level, as did David; and the integrity with which he discharged the functional tasks revealed his character and motivation. Third, David understood that the empowering came from God. At the moment of victory, with Goliath dead and the Philistines in ignominious flight, David remained humble and unostentatious. Humility, so scarce a commodity today in

Christian circles, has always been a characteristic of those who achieve significant things for God. It was true in David's day; it is equally true today. So the biblical paradigm provided in 1 Samuel 17 gives several important insights into the shaping of a famous Old Testament character, but what is the evidence of revival history, for example, regarding the shaping of a potential leader? For the answer to this intriguing question, we can turn to a second source of information and illustration.

Modern material on revival

From the vast amount of information available today, it would appear that men and women God has used have had at least ten common characteristics, although obviously they varied in intensity and strength from individual to individual. They

1. Often had little external attraction; their physical comeliness (or not!) was not their primary feature. This isn't to deny the grace that physical beauty illustrates, rather that God does not wish anything to hinder or obscure his work. The apostle Paul was in person unimpressive, but he was a mighty man of God.

2. Come from no stereotypical background: Zinzendorf was an aristocrat, while Christian David, his fellow worker in Saxony, was a carpenter. John Wesley, Charles Wesley and George Whitefield were all highly educated, but Billy Bray, the Cornish miner, had barely received any education at all.

3. Were often dismissed or nonentites by other men unqualified in the eyes of men. One critic said of Evan Roberts that he was 'too unassuming to claim anything like leadership'.

4. Took prayer seriously. The nineteenth-century revival in New York began with Jeremiah Lanphier calling a prayer meeting in Fulton Street for businessmen in downtown

New York. Six months later 10,000 businessmen were praying for revival; and within two years it is estimated that two million converts were added to the church. One of the greatest examples of prayer in revival history is Robert Murray McCheyne, who prayed: 'Lord, make me as holy as a saved sinner can be.'[41] Similarly John Wesley and George Whitefield were men of prayer.

5. Maintained a close and intimate walk with God. They were people who, in Brian Edwards' memorable phrase, 'were saturated with God'.

6. Had known a life-transforming experience of God. In 1737, George Whitefield prayed, 'God, give me a deep humility, a well-guided zeal, a burning love and a single eye, and then let men or devils do their worst.'[42] In response, he entered into a life-changing experience with God that led to radical developments in his life and ministry.

7. Were humble and realistic in their assessment of themselves and their abilities; not at all proud.

8. Had a passionate desire for God. John Wesley wrote in 1734, 'My one aim in life is to secure personal holiness, for without being holy myself I cannot promote real holiness in others.'[43] And that was even before his conversion, which famously occurred on 23 May 1738.

9. Read and studied the Bible diligently. It is claimed Jonathan Goforth, who was used greatly by God in China at the start of the twentieth century, read through his Chinese New Testament fifty-five times in nineteen years.

10. Were obedient to the Bible. For men and women who lead significant Christian movements, this is a cardinal principle in their lives. Jonathan Edwards, John Wycliffe and Peter Waldo come readily to mind. In reality, characteristics 9 and 10 are inseparable because there is very little purpose in building up mere knowledge of the

Bible; it has to be enacted in our daily lives or else it remains an academic pursuit only.

Which of these characteristics and qualities may, without exaggeration or hagiography, be applied to John and Carol Arnott? In extensive interviews conducted with colleagues or former colleagues, it is possible to identify several key characteristics. They

1. Had served God for many years before the Toronto outpouring. They had planted two churches before 1994, but also had experience of various Christian denominations prior to that date. They were also of mature age, with grown up children.

2. Do not have an inflated view of their own abilities and suitability for leadership. In fact, as has already been shown, they did not consider themselves to be, in any sense, qualified to lead a significant move of God. Disarmingly, John told one Christian journalist that they just told pastors to go home and do what they were doing; if they could do it, anyone could. In the same interview, they were asked how their unexpected high profile had affected their life, to which John replied: that mostly they were out of touch with it – he said they just liked hanging around (with other pastors).

3. Are possessed of considerable reserves of determination and perseverance. They are dogged in pursuing what God has called them to do, in which pursuit they are convinced that God is with them.

4. Have proved God for themselves in the past, coping with failure and also a great deal of personal criticism and hurtful invective: and also, of course, in the experience of marital failure.

5. Are ordinary people, and not particularly well-educated either. This ordinariness has been an advantage to them, enabling them to relate to other ordinary men and women

with transparency and openness in an unthreatening way. John often says, 'We try to be transparent, we have nothing to hide. The Lord prompts me gently to tell it like it is. It keeps you humble and God puts a high value on humility.'

6. Take prayer seriously and spend many hours each week 'soaking' in God's presence. In addition, they read the Bible avidly and desire to put it into practice in their daily lives. In these ways too, John and Carol constantly desire intimacy with God. For them, it is definitely worship and a godly walk before work; and it is out of a deep understanding of God that they preach and minister.

7. Have servant hearts, their desire being to be a blessing to the church as the body of Christ. Stuart Bell, leader of the New Life Christian Fellowship, Lincoln, records these impressions of John and Carol: 'I found them to be very unassuming and honest people, who I sensed have a great compassion for those who are hurting. They spent hours praying for people, and consistently made themselves available to serve.'[44] Willingness to serve is crucial to all that John and Carol do. They serve, not to reveal themselves but, through the Holy Spirit, to reveal the Father to men and women, many of whom are hurting or feel disenfranchised in some way. Their service too reveals their hearts of love and compassion.

Highlighting the above qualities does not mean that John and Carol are flawless – John Wimber referred many years ago to 'leaders with a limp', the possession of which presumably being the antidote to crass arrogance or pride. But the fact remains that the Arnotts have a godly character, exhibit the fruits of the Spirit on Mondays just as they do on Sundays; there is a consistency about their Christian walk which bears scrutiny; and it is a fact that even the most robust – or indeed gruff – opponents of the Toronto Blessing have refrained from attacking their integrity and transparent honesty as people. Proof of their sterling characters is also demonstrated by the way the team at TACF respect John and Carol. The fellow leaders are impressed in particular with the way John sees potential and giftings in other people, and 'is prepared to release them to be the best, even if that liberating process means that they go elsewhere to pursue their ministries' (Mary-Audrey Raycroft), as a number of men and women have done. It was also made clear to the author in conversation with Mary-Audrey that John has an unconscious authority; he does not need to dominate or manipulate, while Carol too is regarded as a leader by other staff members. John is the ultimate visionary, although the negative side of this is that he occasionally rushes into action without first considering carefully enough the administrative and procedural implications.

But it has not all been plain sailing in their pastoral leadership. At Stratford (Ontario), an independent church planted by them in the early 1980s, they saw God move in wonderful ways but, sadly, they did not continue in that vein. John and Carol reacted by restricting all prayer in the meetings to themselves alone. John was sufficiently honest and realistic in his comment: 'We effectively killed what had begun as a definite move of the Spirit, but we determined that we would not repeat that error. We also determined that if God gave us a second chance we would not restrict him so as to make us feel comfortable.' Clearly this was one way in which the Holy Spirit prepared them for the events of January 1994.

Inevitably too, the Toronto church reflects much of the character and make-up of John and Carol, a point David Campbell makes in *By Their Fruits*. He says

> John is a naturally loving sort of man . . . His gentle firmness, genuine humility and clear thinking have influenced all that happens at TACF and kept it safe from being carried away by its own success. I don't think I have ever met anyone more alive in the Spirit than Carol Arnott . . . I believe that Carol's role in keeping the river fresh and full of godly fun, is one of the great-unsung triumphs of the Father's blessing at Toronto.[45]

High praise indeed, which Jack Taylor, a prominent Southern Baptist minister, formerly vice-president of that denomination, puts in a slightly different way in *Experience the Blessing*: 'John and Carol Arnott, amid the rushing of this river of blessings and under a continuous barrage of criticism, have maintained a level of integrity and balance that has helped to protect and sustain a mighty work of God.'

Revivals don't come cheap, however, nor did the sort of leadership sketchily referred to above. For a fuller insight into the experiences and influences that shaped John and Carol in preparation for their life's work, let's turn to a narrative of their lives pre-the Toronto Blessing.

John's story

John Arnott was born on 25 December 1940 when the Second World War was raging in all its awful intensity, destructiveness and loss of life. He was the only son of John Thomas Matthews Arnott and Hazel Louise Turner. Both parents were born in Toronto, though John's paternal grandfather hailed originally from the East End of London, a tough, no-nonsense area, with considerable determination needed merely to survive. His maternal grandparents too came originally from England – George Turner from Sussex, and Evelyn Smith from the Midlands, then the industrial heartland of Britain.

These strong links with Britain have been enhanced by the many visits John and Carol have made since January 1994. There is an additional dimension too as Lori, John's eldest daughter, lives in Birmingham. It's interesting to note that more people from Britain have visited Toronto than from other countries, with the exception of America (and, obviously, Canada!).

In his Foreword to *By Their Fruits*, which chronicles 'The Lasting Impact of Toronto in the UK', John expresses his sense of indebtedness to those men and women who have travelled to Toronto: 'the hungry, the desperate, the discouraged and the sceptical. . . . they came searching for greater anointing, more power, or greater success in ministry'. Instead what they found, or more correctly rediscovered, was 'closeness and intimacy with a loving heavenly Father'. He is also encouraged by the fact that so many Christians in Britain are still hungering and thirsting for a national awakening which, as yet, has not happened.

Toronto based

John Arnott's life has been centred in or near the city of Toronto since birth, with the exception of brief periods of time in Florida. A bustling, cosmopolitan city, dubbed the 'New York of Canada', it has been close to his heart throughout his life, both in terms of business opportunities and church life. He finds it an exciting city, which is also the backdrop to his friendship with Benny Hinn, the well-known evangelist.

His Christian life dates back to 1955: 'I received Jesus at a Billy Graham crusade when I was a young boy. My grandfather saw me standing there with white knuckles and asked if I shouldn't go down to the altar, too. I did and gave my heart to Jesus. Suddenly I realised that I had him in my heart.' Conversion is a defining moment for all who experience it and John, in his meetings, always invites men and women to respond to the call of the gospel. He also has the very highest respect and admiration for Dr Billy Graham.

John's family frequently use the words 'dogged' and 'busy' to describe his lifestyle, qualities which are probably the result of genetic influence and by the very fact of being reared and brought up in a city where determination and success are both highly prized.

In terms of Christian leadership, they also refer to him as an enterprising man, prepared to take risks with people and projects. Not that he's naïve or unrealistic, rather the fact that, with the insight of a visionary, he will pursue objectives and strategies that less adventurous men would recoil from. In *By Their Fruits*, Steve Hepden encapsulates this as his 'entrepreneurial spirit'. This was especially in evidence in his leadership of the church in Stratford where he initiated a scheme for good, low cost housing through a Christian association. This venture combined business acumen and social concern, together with the willingness to take risks. Not all his ventures have been equally successful, but it is an important insight into his character and make-up in general terms of personality and outlook. John is never satisfied with the status quo, and he is constantly looking for the next strategy or initiative that will extend God's kingdom.

Education

John attended the Ontario Bible College for three years, 1966–69, but left without graduating. It is nicely ironic therefore that as a result of his leadership of the Toronto Blessing, he (and Carol) were recently awarded doctorates. Fully entitled therefore to refer to themselves as recipients of this degree, they never refer to this fact because it isn't important to them. What is important is bringing people under the sound and influence of the gospel of good news, so that lives can be transformed and ennobled. John's course at Ontario Bible College emphasised one of the great priorities for all Christians whether in leadership or not – the high value of reading consistently and obeying the Scriptures. It is a central plank in his teaching and preaching, which is why the caricature of the Toronto Blessing as 'no Bible, no cross, no preaching etc.' is not only ludicrous but also inadequate and unhelpful.

However the theological studies at Ontario Bible College did not lead to any form of pastoral leadership, and John pursued a number of business opportunities, including a travel business, property speculation, and a flower shop, which was eventually bought by his mother. Pastoral ministry remained, however, the primary desire of his life, although it was over a decade into the future before it was realised, and not before he had undergone distressing personal failure.

Falling apart

Failure to complete his academic and theological studies was followed within six years by an even more traumatic event: divorce. John's first marriage ended tragically in divorce due to irreconcilable differences. Those who have experienced divorce will readily appreciate that it is an anxious, frequently debilitating and stressful process. John was no exception, and he found this time in his life destructive, frustrating, and angst-ridden. It was also, of course, a painful reminder of his own parents' divorce (later, after his father had come back to God after a period of backsliding, they were reconciled but did not remarry).

Inner healing, one of the central emphases of John's ministry today, was desperately needed, but it was to be four years before 'Carol literally loved me back to life. People today describe us as a loving couple – it flowed from Carol originally.' Carol was able to empathise with John because she too had experienced the pain of separation and divorce, when her husband deserted her for another woman. God has a way of redeeming personal failures, and both John and Carol have gone on to positive and productive lives since they separated from their first partners. Their lives prove that failure does not, of necessity, disqualify in God's kingdom.

Divorce, odd though it may sound to the Christian community, had beneficial effects on both John and Carol in terms of their general character and understanding of people. First it made them deeply sympathetic to the dilemmas and tragedies that blight the lives of men and women, both pastors and lay people. They are able to enter into other people's sufferings precisely because they, themselves, have faced rejection and the scorn of others. Second it inculcated in them a sense of humility. Third it taught them that problems must be confronted if wholeness is to be achieved and sustained. Fourth their respective divorces offered a stark alternative: 'When life falls apart,' says Carol, 'people can either get better or bitter.' This encomium can possibly be seen as a simplistic comment but it is one which is grounded in the reality of everyday life for both John and Carol. It has also meant that their response to other people similarly experiencing divorce is sympathetic and understanding. It has also kept them humble and realistic.

Dwarfing all these considerations, however, is the fact that their relationship, its mutual respect and deep love, has been crucial to the success of their pastoral leadership. They work as a team, deferring to each other, encouraging, motivating, and mutually desiring the best for each other. This emotionally fulfilling relationship helped to restore confidence and security, after a bleak time of recrimination in both failed marriages; and it has been a rich source of encouragement for other Christian couples going through similarly distressing circumstances. Only equals can submit to each other, something John and Carol do willingly. John clearly has greater administrative authority in terms of TACF's organisation and administration, but he has encouraged Carol in ministry, and she frequently admits, in public, her profound debt and gratitude to John for fostering her preaching gift. As one fellow leader said at the tenth 'Catch The Fire' conference in 2003, 'One could never have imagined Carol preaching like she did this time ten years ago.' A transformation indeed. On the other hand, it would not be valid to present the healing process alluded to above as either easy or rapid, and it took time for John, whose confidence had suffered a severe battering, to recover emotionally and spiritually. Recover he did though, and it is perhaps difficult when seeing this cuddly, personable man speaking with such quiet assurance and authority in public gatherings, to imagine a time when his life was falling part in such a dramatic way. But fall apart it did, as he would be the first to recognise and admit.

Lori

John has two daughters from his first marriage. Lori was born on 3 August 1962, and Vicki on 25 May 1964. Lori recalls becoming a Christian at the tender age of three, with John himself leading her gently to faith in Jesus Christ. She clearly remembers it as a 'solemn occasion, accompanied too by crying'. Nine years later, she was baptised in the Holy Spirit, and frequently attended healing meetings conducted by Kathryn Kuhlman, who attracted enormous audiences in the 1960s with her dramatic form of evangelism. She operated primarily on receiving 'words of knowledge' concerning the physical condition of people in the congregation, and many were instantly healed as a consequence. John Arnott's thinking was deeply influenced by Kuhlman.

Now in her early forties, and with children of her own, Lori has vivid and affectionate memories of her father reading Bible stories to her, to which she responded with a multiplicity of questions and eager inquiries. In this way, John laid down for Lori a firm biblical basis for both faith and behaviour. Lori's other memories of John as a father include his stubbornly-held belief that all games, whether football, baseball or ice hockey, were fixed and decided beforehand. This viewpoint inevitably led to John's rather dismissive perspective on professional, competitive sport, an attitude he retains to this day. In contrast, he was much more interested in household gadgets and holidays in Florida, preferences which, again, he holds to this day!

Testimonies

Lori has distinct, vivid, impressions from an early age, of the way her father conducted public meetings. He always had a passion for 'testimony-driven meetings'.

These testimonies would allow men and women to identify and describe what God had done for them in terms of the significant changes in their lives; and also how their life experiences had helped them to understand his ways more clearly. Such positive changes, and even the difficult times, are considered by John to be worth sharing with other people, so that they can be encouraged and built up in their faith. John views the testimonies of people as a 'spur' to seek more of God's infilling love and power. Lori fully concurs with her father's perspective in this respect. John's attitude is reminiscent of the great Methodist leader, John Wesley, who would spend great tracts of time avidly listening to individuals' accounts of God's dealings with them. At this point too it is worth recalling Jeff Lucas' pertinent comment in *Grace Choices*

> Perhaps we need to rediscover what used to be called 'the testimony time', which largely fell into disuse because dear old Doris was always thanking God for healing her chilblains (which seemed to come back on Monday morning, must have been the devil) or because young Pete tended to drop a swearword into his testimony every time he took the microphone. But in a world

apparently obsessed with reality television and in order that we can truly discover God's beauty in each other, the church must be courageous and break the notion that truth is only to be handled by the ordained and trained professionals.'[46]

Releasing the power of what Lucas calls 'community hermeneutics' has always been a crucial part of John Arnott's conducting of public meetings.

The Toronto model in this respect has not earned universal approval, but John remains convinced that testimonies have a vital and helpful rôle to play, a conviction he holds to tenaciously for another reason. As he explains in his Introduction to *Experience the Blessing*, 'You need to know that the fresh and powerful experiences of the Holy Spirit . . . are way beyond anything most of us have ever seen before. Carol and I are constantly redirecting the attention of people away from the look of the manifestations and onto the fruit in the person's life . . . If God really touches us, even a little, the miracle is that we live to tell the story.'[47]

Lori is unequivocal in viewing John as 'a good father if somewhat distant', although she accepts that the reason for this distance is the fact that John's own parents split up when he was aged eighteen, thus he lacked an appropriate rôle-model. Inevitably too, John has been less immediately available since 1994, but he continues to be, in her view, a concerned and caring father and grandfather. He wishes, for example, that Lori would return to reside in Canada, a wish that remains, as yet, unfulfilled. She remembers too that her parents divorce was an extremely difficult time for both John and his first wife. 'I knew,' she says, 'that I had to remain with my father whereas Vicki opted to stay with my mother.'

Qualities
What, in Lori's view were her father's qualities? She perceives him as

- active and a visionary – not a dreamer; full of bright ideas
- adventurous, with a definite sense of fun
- determined and persevering

- genuine, with integrity and honesty marked features of his dealings with her and her own children
- firmly grounded in reality, both in his personal and church lives. She perceived that there was no dichotomy between his behaviour in church and that outside it. It was a seamless tapestry which she hugely appreciated.

Sometimes costly

Lori offers one final recollection. She vividly recalls that in January 1994, John simply said: 'Get here.' She was impressed, and remains so to this day, by his sense of excitement – wonder would not be too strong a word to use – at what God was doing. It was, in her opinion, an innocent, almost naïve reaction to an event he had been waiting for all his Christian life. She knows that John and Carol see it as a remarkable privilege to pastor the outbreak of the Holy Spirit in Toronto; and Lori herself accedes to the perception that it is 'truly a Spirit-led revival'. For this reason, she interprets the split with the Vineyard movement to have been 'deeply hurtful' not only for John and Carol, but also for the whole Toronto church. With hindsight, it is clear that the decisions reached towards the end of 1995 and the ensuing controversy caused much heartache in the Arnott household, as it did too to John Wimber. This acute sense of dislocation was felt profoundly by Randy Clark, whose whole future in ministry appeared clouded and uncertain: 'I [also] didn't know whether or not to remain in a Vineyard church. I resolved that I, too, would wait and see how the Vineyard's decision to disfellowship would impact me.' (From *Lighting Fires*.) In the event, it worked out successfully for both Clark and TACF, but no attempt must be made to minimise the anguish John and Carol felt at that time.

It is also important to understand the whole matter of the preparation and the shaping for ministry that had taken place in the lives of John and Carol. During their formative years in Stratford God had taught them, again in Randy Clark's words, 'that the anointing always costs something'. There is ample biblical support for the ideas of submission and sacrifice. True discipleship is not a theoretical idea; it is sometimes costly, not just in terms of finance and time, but crucially it affects all our relationships. John and Carol had imbibed these lessons in comparative obscurity, and so they were able to accept the pain of what was manifestly a sharp disagreement and, also, to carry on with God's call on their lives. And they would have gone on doing so had January 1994 not happened.

Before moving on to the recollections of John's younger daughter, it might be helpful to refer, albeit briefly, to another parting of the ways recorded in the New Testament which like the events referred to above were a cause for considerable concern and no little regret. In Acts 15, Paul and Barnabas disagreed radically over their perceptions of Mark; and both were stubborn in their response because they viewed it as a matter of principle. The upshot of this disagreement was that Barnabas sailed to Cyprus taking with him Mark, while Paul selected Silas as his companion in ministry. Paul's intimate relationship with Barnabas was broken, but their friendship persisted; and later, as the New Testament makes clear they were reconciled and Paul also came to appreciate the sterling qualities in Mark that Barnabas had identified earlier. The biblical analogy is relevant when assessing the split between the Toronto church and the Vineyard movement in at least two ways. First both parties were enabled to go in a direction of their own choosing, with the Toronto church pursuing what was designated as a 'new tributary'. Second both parties retained their mutual respect and admiration for each other without, at any time disguising the reality and intensity of the issues that separated them. Significantly too, many speakers associated with the Vineyard grouping continue to preach and minister at TACF to this day, with Randy Clark and Ed Piorek prominent among them.

Vicki

Vicki now lives in Dallas. She shares her sister's sense of incredulity and shock at her parents divorce: 'I didn't really believe it.' Such a reaction is perfectly understandable, but she is immensely grateful that, wisely and protectively, her parents did everything possible to shield her from the worst of the emotional and practical problems arising from a family split.

Acrimony almost invariably accompanies a divorce, so it is to her parents' credit that common sense and mutual understanding prevailed.

Like her sister, many of Vicki's early memories are related to famous Christian figures, including Kathryn Kuhlman and her dramatic – almost theatrical – presentation of the gospel, but also her real openness to the promptings and guidance of the Holy Spirit. She recalls too Benny Hinn's meetings in Toronto long before he became a famous preacher and flamboyant television personality. Hinn was one of John Arnott's close friends at that time, and John still views him as such, although their differing ministries prevent them from personal contacts on an ongoing basis. Some commentators often point to Hinn as one of the dominant exemplars in the spiritual development of John Arnott. Hinn, in turn, had viewed Kuhlman as one of his exemplars in ministry, and Guy Chevreau (*Catch The Fire*, published by Marshall Pickering in 1994) offers the view that 'in significant ways [Kuhlman and Hinn] laid an imprint for the future direction of [Arnott's] ministry'. Criticism by association is not a valid approach, and much future work, though not within the remit of this book, needs to be done in comparing the theology, hermeneutics, the role of Scripture, and attitude towards the manifestations of the Spirit (reactions to the Holy Spirit), in John and Carol's thinking – all these issues need to be evaluated in open, rational, polemical debate in a manner akin to *The Mark of the Spirit?* Vicki herself is of the opinion that although her father had a close relationship with Hinn back in the 1970s, the guiding principle of his life has been to follow what he perceives – for himself – that the Spirit is saying.

But what was John like as a father from Vicki's perspective? Vicki says that he was a 'loving, touchy-feely father', with whom she had a close and fulfilling relationship, and she looks at the Toronto Blessing as facilitating an even closer relationship with him. 'It has,' she says, 'affected him in that he has grown and developed as a person and as a father. He has also retained his personal humility.' She thinks that John is a patient, kind and generous grandfather. She adds: 'I feel too that I am a better person as a result of the Toronto awakening. At first, the whole experience was a shock to me, even shocking, but the inner healing it has brought (not just to me, of course) and the whole concept of "soaking prayer" has changed me in radical and positive ways.'

Life's experiences – the analogy of a mosaic or tapestry is perhaps pertinent – shape men and women in distinct and definite ways, and Lori and Vicki's recollections, plus those of other people too, are helpful in identifying how John was shaped long before January 1994. Three levels of 'building' are apparent.

First, in terms of character: John possessed qualities of integrity, honesty and humility many years before God called him to lead the church in Toronto. The shattering experience of divorce caused him to think that he was somehow disqualified for leadership in God's kingdom. He did though surmise that he could, at least, help those who had gone through similarly traumatic events of disharmony and separation. Such a humble posture does not go unnoticed by God. And when God called him to lead the Toronto awakening he embraced it enthusiastically and fully, delighting in what God was doing.

Second, in terms of family commitment: His rôle as a father was deeply important to him – which is why his divorce caused such intense heartache – as indeed is his rôle as a grandfather today, although his time is severely restricted as far as purely family occasions are concerned.

From their earliest days, Lori and Vicki were taught the Scriptures systematically and seriously. It was, for John, the rock and foundation of everything in his life, alongside openness to the Spirit. 'The Bible,' he says, 'keeps us from falling into error.' So he taught his children the absolute necessity of lining up their lives, behaviour and relationships with the teaching of the Bible, a point he frequently reiterates in his preaching.

Third, in the understanding that God is the God of the 'second chance'. This principle is most notably illustrated in the life of the Old Testament character Jonah, but John imbibed this lesson in the aftermath to his divorce. At the heart of this principle is, of course, the idea of forgiveness. Wounds, as John often teaches, sap energy and resources in men and women, but forgiveness is the indispensable key to blessing and the fruitful release of God's life in human beings. John teaches that three things are absolutely essential in this process: the need for a revelation of how immense God is, the need to understand and act upon how caring and loving he is, and the need for a revelation so that we can walk in God's love and impart it to other people. We can, and must, treat others with 'grace healed' eyes. This latter requirement is emblazoned on a banner at the back of TACF. It is a mission statement, if you wish, of everything that John has learned both inside and outside church too.

These details have sketched some of the highs and the lows in the first thirty-five years or so of John Arnott's life, both as a Christian and as a husband and father. At the point of his divorce, he felt that everything was 'going down the drain', and in a conversation with journalist Clive Price he commented rather ruefully: 'I ended up with my two daughters kind of looking after dad.' These words are a typically honest admission, though happily, his personal circumstances were not destined to remain in this depressed and bleak state, a transformation brought about to a very large degree by the person who became his second wife: Carol. Let's turn then to the details of her life before she encountered John.

Carol's story

Carol was born on 9 May 1943, the only daughter of Wilfred Bechthold and Florence Hahn. Her birthplace was Milverton, a small, unpretentious town approximately half an hour's drive from Stratford, Ontario. Her parents were born in the Ketchener area but, as their names suggest, were originally of German ancestry. Her father was a railwayman. Home life for Carol was not, however, always harmonious or peaceful. This was largely due to the fact that her mother, Florence, had grown up in a largely rural hard working farm home, with a great deal of hurt and rejection. She had also suffered physical abuse and she, in turn, dealt harshly with Carol when she had committed some minor, childish misdemeanour. Florence would take Wilfred's belt and whack Carol until there were, in her own words, 'black and blue welts on my body'. The deeper hurts were, of course, internal and psychological, and Carol's defence mechanism was to hate her mother: 'Inside I judged her and despised her.' Later, there had to come a time when Carol needed to forgive her mother, but as a young child growing up, that thought did not feature prominently in her mind.

Life moved on, however. She does not consider herself to have been particularly well-educated, and she did not proceed to university after completing her High School years where she followed the equivalent of A-Level studies in England. Instead she became a secretary in a bank, later becoming a legal secretary, a rôle she was comfortable with and also found stimulating. Her naturally friendly, gregarious personality meant that she fitted in easily with the various routines at work and, in addition, she enjoyed a wide-ranging social life.

Life seemed idyllic. She married her 'childhood sweetheart', and the marriage produced two children. Rob, unmarried, is now aged thirty-seven, and lives in Australia where he is the chief executive officer at the research institute attached to the University of Melbourne. He is a Christian, as is his younger brother, Mike, aged thirty-five. He too is unmarried, and is an industrial mechanic. He lives in Stratford, thus in close proximity to Carol, and attends Jubilee Christian Fellowship where John and Carol were the founding pastors.

At this stage she could have been forgiven for thinking that they were all going to live happily ever after. It was not to be, however, and her marriage fell apart after a comparatively brief period of seven years. The blow was doubly distressing and poignant because her husband had deserted her for someone with whom Carol worked. She felt bereft and ashamed, and hardly surprisingly her life, in a mirror image of John's, fell apart almost completely.

As with John, the period of dislocation and divorce was traumatic. She had always taken her marriage vows seriously, believing in its fidelity, sanctity and the permanence of her marriage vows. She felt betrayed and humiliated by her husband's departure, while her sons felt bereft at the absence of their father.

Carol recalls this time as one of 'total chaos'. There followed a time of emotional and psychological abuse, and the police were called as a protective and cautionary strategy. Cumulatively these events were deeply unsettling, and the boys began to be adversely affected.

Mike especially became angry, expressing his frustration inappropriately by destroying personal items belonging to his mother and brother. Clearly he was suffering from depression, and was in need of psychiatric help and counselling. Carol was depressed too.

If she had been asked at this critical stage of her life if she was a Christian, she would have replied affirmatively that she was a 'Christian of the Lutheran persuasion'. What, however, she needed was not a routine inoculation of religion but a supernatural encounter with God: and that's precisely what happened.

Life-transforming event

It came about in this way. She was in the bathroom when she heard a voice speaking in English, which she assumed, in her anxious state, was the voice of her former husband – a natural assumption induced by anguish and distress; such a thought was frightening. In fact, after the voice started and stopped five times, she wondered whether she was on the verge of a nervous breakdown, but she was not.

After a lengthy time, however, the voice started repeating the words of Psalm 23, with its majestic encouragement to those who are truly following God in faith and hope. What was happening?

In response, Carol went to the bottom drawer of her dresser, got out her Confirmation Bible and read the psalm over and over again to herself, still not quite comprehending what was taking place in her life. Eventually she realised that the voice speaking to her directly through the words of Scripture was none other than Jesus, the Son of God and Saviour of the world.

'I understood,' she says, 'that he loved me personally, unreservedly, and that he wanted to deal with all my sin, all my hurt, all my embedded and corrosive anger, and all my past distress.' Above all, perhaps, she understood that Jesus loved her extravagantly and for herself, not for her gifts and abilities, and not even for any future work she might do in his kingdom. This was a startling, even stunning, revelation to her, the wonder of which is as vibrant today as it was then: 'Nothing in my upbringing or past religious life had prepared me for this transforming moment in my life: it was the preparation, although I did not appreciate it at that time, for my later ministry role in communicating the love of God to hurting men and women all over the world.'

This rôle was, of course, far into the future, but for Carol the release and relief was immediate and palpable: she felt it at the deepest levels of her being and personality. She remembers skipping around the local shops saying rapturously, 'the Lord is my shepherd, I shall not want'! She now felt full of the life and love of God, although, as yet, she did not appreciate conceptually or theologically the nature of the experience. It did not conform to any formula and prescribed evangelical method of becoming a Christian; still, she could speak in terms of 'entering into new life in Christ'. She had indeed been surprised by joy. In fact, the joy was unbounded; a feeling that increased the following month when in their living room, kneeling on the carpet, she led both boys in a simple prayer to ask Jesus to forgive their sins and come into their hearts and be their Lord and Saviour. Mike was totally healed in that moment and never went back to the doctor's again, and has been loving Jesus ever since.

Support and encouragement

The helpfulness of Christian neighbours too was important and strengthening for Carol at this time of change in her life. They constantly looked after her in a pastoral sense for the next two years, including asking her to attend meetings convened by Kathryn Kuhlman. At these meetings further shocks were in store for her as she witnessed the supernatural healing of a boy with callipers, which he dramatically removed from his weakened and atrophied legs. At this moment too, Kathryn called out someone in the choir being healed of a back ailment, at which point Carol stood up and promptly fell over. Her back was healed. She was similarly wide-eyed with amazement when a disabled lady was healed on the platform.

The significance of these events for Carol cannot be over-estimated. She was being introduced to Jesus the Healer, on the one hand, and the powerful Holy Spirit, on the other. These twin emphases continue to characterise her ministry to this day. The Holy Spirit had not been a 'real' person to her previously, simply a disembodied spirit who had no particular power or dynamism in the contemporary world, but here she was being introduced personally to the Holy Spirit. This was not through systematic teaching but directly and experientially; and seeing the Spirit move in this way touched Carol deeply, convincing her that he really was on earth carrying on the work of Jesus: in conviction, salvation and sanctification. This new-found awareness was an integral part of Carol's shaping for January 1994 and onwards.

The immediacy and speed of Carol's baptism in the Holy Spirit contrasted with the slower, more leisurely entry of John Arnott into the same experience. He had prayed to God for at least a year, but 'nothing, nothing, nothing seemed to happen'. Then: 'One night, in the middle of a spiritual dream, I felt like a volcano went off inside of me and I ended up saying a sentence or two in unknown tongues, but the sheer nearness of it overwhelmed me.' This was not merely an 'emotional experience', as his pastor tried to explain it to him, because John now felt entirely different: 'Whereas before God seemed to [be] millions of miles away, now he felt right there with me.' That's exactly how Carol felt too.

Rites of passage

Reflecting on Carol's experience thus far, the salient markers are these: home life (less than satisfactory in some ways), a fairly ordinary education, followed by a fulfilling administrative job, romantic illusions of marriage (and they all lived happily ever after) destroyed by her experiences as her first marriage broke down, the falling apart of her life (as John's had done), and a supernatural meeting with God. The dimension not subsumed into the list above is how to place the difficult and traumatic experiences into the context of Christian leadership.

Christian leaders, it is erroneously assumed, are flawless individuals, though this is not Carol's perception at all. She contends that all leaders have – or have had – problems of various sorts: all are scarred, albeit in diverse ways and to varying degrees of intensity, by life's complexities and tragedies. When problems occur they can become 'bitter or better', but the interesting feature of Carol Arnott's life is that she had to decide not to be bitter before assuming the mantle of leadership because of her first husband's unreasonable behaviour. In reality it was a potential stumbling-block that became a fruitful stepping-stone when she was called to leadership with John following their marriage in 1979.

A question of forgiveness

Not everything was plain sailing for Carol after her conversion. A complex issue presented itself immediately, involving the matter of forgiveness in relation to her mother. The roots of this issue, in reality, extended far back into Carol's mother's own upbringing. Florence had been the youngest of seven children, and the fifth daughter, in a hard-working farming family. With only two sons to cope with the burden of hard, unremitting physical labour, the family inevitably and understandably wished for another boy, so Carol's mother was neither wanted nor welcomed. The treatment meted out to her lacked all kindness and sensitivity, still less tenderness, as Carol explains: 'Since my mother's parents often worked in the fields, her sisters were expected to raise her. But kids being kids – and perhaps not very well mothered either – they were often cruel to her. They would rock her violently in her cradle. When she cried as a little toddler, they would lock her in a closet for hours at a time.'

Today such psychological and physical ill-treatment is widely castigated, though at the time Florence was a child, less attention was paid to the ways in which children were reared.

So Carol's mother endured the pain of rejection, injustice, control and domination and what would be termed today as physical abuse. Out of her inner hurt Florence would punish Carol with undue and unnecessary severity, and often her body would be scarred and painful after being subjected to essentially inhuman treatment.

Internal scars were potentially more serious, and Carol hated her mother, despised her, and thus a huge deposit of unforgiveness was built up inside her emotionally. The problem was not dealt with easily or quickly. Three years before Carol forgave her mother in her head, and only after concentrated teaching from John and Paula Sandford, the internationally known Christian teachers on inner healing. They showed her that there are two equally significant sides to forgiveness. One is the need to forgive; the other is the need to repent of the sin of judging and dishonouring [Duet 5:16] the other person. As Carol candidly admits, 'I had forgiven my mother, but on the other hand, I didn't honour her in my heart. I hated and judged her.'

That process of judging was Carol's sin, not her mother's; and only after a period of teaching, counselling, and several negative responses from her mother, was the situation eventually resolved. One day Carol was about to leave her mother's house when she hugged her and told Florence that that she loved her. As she said goodbye, a surprising and wonderful love for her mother welled up in her heart: 'I knew I was healed. I knew that God had done a work in my heart.' Both John and Carol needed to forgive those who had hurt them, or betrayed their trust, and the fruits of those events affecting both of them are reflected and analysed in John's booklet, *The Importance of Forgiveness*.[48]

Pertinent and revealing questions

John and Carol are frequently asked such questions as 'Who are you?', 'What did you do to bring the outpouring about?', 'How did it alter the focus of your ministry?', 'What has impacted you most about the Toronto Blessing?', 'Is it revival?', 'What will it lead to?'. That such questions need to be asked, especially perhaps the first two, indicates that they are ordinary people with no desire for publicity or media exposure. They are self-admittedly ordinary human beings where personal gifts and abilities are concerned, but they are extraordinary in their devotion to, and love for, God as their heavenly Father; and in this relationship there is confidence and reassurance.

Both speak quietly and respond to questions in a restrained and, in John's case, understated way. This impressed Scott McDermott when he questioned John about the controversies surrounding the manifestations and work of the Holy Spirit: 'I was able to ask John about this aspect of his ministry. His response was not defensive. Instead, he [made] it clear that these physical responses were not his focus, nor was he encouraging these responses. He was more concerned with the changes that [take] place in a person's life than with the appearance of his or her encounter with God. It was a reasonable response.'[49]

Ordinary they may be, but clearly God saw personal qualities of character and temperament in John and Carol that he could use in leadership. Brian Edwards, in *Revival*, makes this discerning comment: 'In revival, God will frequently use those who are unqualified in the eyes of men.' How true, and also easily illustrated from a historical perspective.

One of the most appropriate examples to cite is Evan Roberts, An unlikely hero if ever there was one: largely uneducated, unassuming in terms of personality, certainly not an extrovert, his daily job before the Welsh Revival 1904–05 was in a blacksmith's forge. Not exactly a prime candidate to lead a worldwide movement, but God apparently was not interested in Roberts' lack of education or unsophisticated ways: he perceived in him a willingness to be obedient. Evan Roberts did not become a leader through denominational success (he was not an ordained minister, in any case), or by strength of character, or by organising ability, or by dedication to unremitting work – rather because the 'mark of God's spirit' (Brian Edwards' notable phrase) was upon him. Prior to the revival too, he had met with God in a life-transforming way, and from the intimacy of God's presence he was equipped to lead a revival while, at the same time, remaining self-effacing and unfailingly humble. R.B. Jones, in *Rent Heavens,* says: 'One of the characteristics of true Revival is that it depends on no human personality. It is never organised; it is never, so to speak, carried in any individual's pocket.'[50]

Clearly no attempt is being made here to draw an analogy between the Arnotts and Evan Roberts, apart from pointing out that they too are humble and willing to obey God's directives. They are also people who love God's immediate presence, and have a passionate love for Jesus.

It is also possible to conclude that their lives were shaped in particular ways under God's guidance, personally, biblically and pastorally, in preparation for the many roles they now fulfil. To these aspects of God's shaping must also be added their marriage, which took place in 1979.

1979–94: Key developments

John and Carol's marriage has been – and is – enormously successful: they are friends in addition to being married. They complement each other; and support and encourage each other in a relationship that seems to be devoid of competitiveness and striving, and they work harmoniously together, especially when ministering together. Theirs is a rock-solid marriage; and their love and respect for each other is manifest, both in public and in private. Their second marriage has been a fruitful source of healing for them both: emotional order and confidence were restored almost at once. As John said, 'Everything turned for the better'; neither exhibits the bitterness that almost invariably accompanies divorce.

The years from 1979–94 were extremely busy. In addition to business and church activities, there were four teenage children to look after. In 1980, while on a combined business and ministry trip to Indonesia, John responded to God's call on his life to full-time ministry. Soon after, they felt in the words of a close associate, that 'they wanted to move their vocational commitments from business to the work of ministry.' They did this and, in mid-June 1981, planted their first church, Jubilee Christian Ministries (later Jubilee Vineyard, but since 1995

Jubilee Christian Fellowship), in Stratford, Ontario, some ninety miles west of Toronto. Its first location was actually a farmhouse just south of Stratford. There were twenty-four people at their first meeting, consisting mostly of close friends of John and Carol, and including Carol's mother and father. When John and Carol were first called to full-time ministry, the example of David (recounted in 1 Sam. 22:1,2) was especially encouraging to them: David's mighty army, his men of valour, began as a small group of friends and relatives gathered together in a cave. In the early days part of Jubilee's reputation was that it attracted couples, particularly young people, who would not otherwise have attended an established church. This was true, but then Jesus' command in Luke 14:23, 'Go out into the highways and hedges and compel them to come in, that my house may be filled' (KJV), led to a wider and further outreach, and after just a few weeks in the farmhouse Jubilee moved to the Optimist Hall where Sunday evening services were started, which occasionally included the showing of Christian films. Quickly outgrowing the Optimist Hall, the church moved into first Avon, then Shakespeare, schools.

An independent charismatic church, it took its name from the year of freedom described in the Old Testament. According to several people, the name was perfectly suited to the leadership of John and Carol. This freedom was evident personally – many were saved, healed and delivered – and also on a corporate level, as John encouraged extravagant worship, the flow of the Holy Spirit, and opportunities for many people to lead the services. God showed John that a place was needed where new Christians could simply 'hang out' together and enjoy normal, everyday friendship, and so the church was transferred to a former pool hall in downtown Stratford. Several pool tables were retained by the church, which opened as a drop-in centre during the week, and was frequented by drug addicts and others whose lives were broken, or in significant ways dysfunctional. Many of these people came to know Jesus Christ and their lives were changed for the better: evangelism has always been at the forefront of the Arnotts' vision. The former pool hall premises were known as 'The Upper Rooms', and in the early days there one of the guest speakers was Benny Hinn. 'Christian Bikers' too held a service in The Upper Rooms.

These were exciting times, and the church's ministry expanded in other directions too with the establishment of a Christian school, Jubilee Academy, in September 1983. Four years later, in 1987, Jubilee received an invitation to join the Association of Vineyard Churches, following an application made the previous year. In response to a vision God gave John at this time, other Vineyard churches were planted, including the Barrie Vineyard, Scarborough Vineyard, and the Thornhill Vineyard. At this time, John Wimber's influence was pervasive and powerful, and the Arnotts felt privileged to be part of the network Wimber led with such humour and humanity.

Leadership qualities

But what specifically were John and Carol like as leaders? Jeff Duncan, now a worship leader in the Guelph Vineyard Church, Ontario, was one of the young men trained and schooled by John, eventually becoming the senior worship leader at Jubilee for approximately five years. Here are his recollections of that formative period in his life, and in that of the fledgling church.

> The church grew rapidly under John's leadership. His leadership style balanced authority with grace and determination with a relaxed easy-going attitude. A visionary, he was never content with the status-quo, and was determined to provoke change. His big teddy-bear demeanour almost always won people over. His preaching style was always inspiring and easy to listen to; though impressed as I was with what he said, what he didn't say left a bigger impression on me. Let me explain.
>
> John was always getting other people to speak, whether it was guest speakers or those of us from the pews. The constant stream of guest speakers and ordinary folk talking from the pulpit made the Jubilee church an exciting place to be. We never knew what to expect next, which could have been unsettling, but the benefits far outweighed the risks.

John encouraged us to share a testimony or preach, often before we felt ready. It seemed his modus operandi was 'you can do it'; and he was always challenging us to go beyond our comfort zones, to do the works of the kingdom, to be leaders. He was a remarkable man who was motivated to see others grow and be fruitful. John's ability to train and release leaders has produced dozens of leaders who today are in many capacities of leadership all around the world.

Jeff Duncan also provides an excellent insight into the Arnotts' way of dealing with potentially complex problems and difficulties. On one occasion when Jeff was in his twenties he prophesied to a young lady about some things he believed God was saying. She apparently agreed with him, but then complained to John and Carol about him. Their response was to go to prayer about the whole matter, asking God to show them why Jeff should have behaved in the way he did.

Issues clarified and resolved
A few weeks later, they invited Jeff and his wife over for a meal.

Afterwards John told me about the error I had made in prophesying and then said that they believed God had shown them a reason for my error: deep rejection. As we talked and prayed, we came to realise that when I had first become baptised in the Holy Spirit, I had experienced huge rejection from my family, my spiritual mentor and my Christian peers, who had, in fact, rejected my experience as either emotionalism or, even worse, the work of the devil. My response to this rejection was a determination to show my family, my mentor and my peers and the whole world that the gifts of the Holy Spirit were for today. Having such wrong motives for using the gifts of the Spirit had caused me to be out of balance and had left the door open for the devil to deceive me. That day John and Carol's healing prayer unlocked a flood of revelation and healing, and I began to see that I had become a zealot for all the wrong reasons. In John and Carol's living-room that day, after repenting of my vows and from my lifestyle of seeking people's approval, I received the Father's approval and I was healed of my rejection.

That day was a decisive turning-point in Jeff's life. In the passage of time, his family, personal and church lives were put in order, largely because of the prayerful and sensitive manner in which John and Carol brought correction to him. This necessary correction also brought healing; and instead of being crushed by the heavy hand of discipline, he felt loved and encouraged, not only to learn an important lesson, but to 'fly' again. He also understood the importance of hearing God's voice before administering correction. An additional minor point needs to be referred to: they served Jeff in their home instead of calling him formally and officially to the church office. This was another valuable lesson Jeff has never forgotten.

But Jeff was not the only one to learn vitally important lessons: Carol did too. She found that people would complain to her, but not to John, if they felt hurt or rejected or neglected in some way. To Carol's annoyance, John seemed unable or unwilling to defend her; and she noticed the same pattern when they started the church in Toronto. She was particularly annoyed and frustrated when John sought to explain the problem in terms of her behaviour, not theirs: 'You are over-reacting again,' was sometimes his response. Then she realised that she had judged her father for not standing up to her mother's unfairly aggressive behaviour to her as a child, and now those judgements 'gave the enemy legal rights that resulted in the primary man in my life, John, not being able to protect me from "mother" church'. She also understood at this time that the only route to follow was to forgive her father and John for not defending her. And the result? In her own words: 'Two months later there was another incident. A lady came to me and dumped a lot of nasty stuff on me. I went to John, and immediately he said, "We are going to call her in to my office." He called her in, stood up for me and dealt with the situation. It was amazing. He has been the same way ever since.' Problem solved.

Over six years after planting the church in Stratford, John and Carol started a home group (also known as a kinship group) in west Toronto, which met in John's mother's living room. Then, in May 1988, they established a second church in Toronto. By this time, the Stratford church had become officially a Vineyard church. Both churches grew in numbers, with John and Carol commuting between them.

Summer 1992

The summer of 1992 was a most important time for John and Carol, for several different reasons.

In July 1992, they began pastoring the Toronto church full-time, having turned the Stratford church over to an associate, Jerry Steingard. Soon they were joined in a full-time capacity by Jeremy and Connie Sinnott, who now assumed responsibility for the worship side of the church's activities. This was, and is, a fruitful relationship, with all four people working harmoniously together. It is, as Jeremy says, one based on mutual trust and respect; and Jeremy characterises the Arnotts as 'supernaturally natural' in their dealings with people. Jeremy also says: 'What you see in John and Carol is who and what they are.'

Glimpses into the future

In retrospect, it is clear that the shaping of their lives and ministry was speeding up, and in the summer of 1992 they were given a foretaste of later events from 1994 onwards. John invited Clive Corfield, an English pastor, to minister at the Stayner Family Camp under the auspices of the Canadian Vineyard. This he did, but on his night off Marc Dupont (close associate of TACF) declared: 'God wants to minister to leaders.' Clive went to the front where Carol Arnott said: 'Clive, tonight's your night.' With that he fell to the floor, laughing uncontrollably and also crying. He tried to get up but couldn't, by which time the preacher was being introduced. Clive felt as if invisible hands were holding him down. The speaker tried to speak, then said, 'get that guy [meaning Clive] out of here.' Clive was eventually carried out, but by now his wife was crying at the apparent disgrace caused by her husband. In fact, he laughed all night and because he was too drunk to drive, had to be driven back to Toronto by someone else. This was a forerunner of what subsequently happened at TACF. Those near to Clive as he laughed and cried were astounded at the sight of an Englishman (normally known for their phlegmatic, controlled and unexcitable ways!) behaving in such a manner. Very soon, of course, such behaviour was common at TACF, and from 1994 had worldwide reverberations. Clive considers the Toronto Blessing to be a unique and deeply significant move of the Holy Spirit, imparting new life and energy to pastors and ordinary people alike.

Back at John and Carol's church a ministry team was quickly established, but this aspect of the church did not work out as perhaps the Arnotts had anticipated. John honestly admits that they had run dry in ministering in the way they had been. The reasons for this dryness are explained in *Keep The Fire*

> We had a significant 'hospital' in our church – people whom we spent a lot of time counselling and working on inner healing and deliverance. People were maturing and changing. It was wonderful, but it took two or three years – or even longer – for people to become relatively free inside. We always saw something else that needed to be done. Our focus was on the people, the troubles and the healings needed instead of the Lord. To us, it became as though the devil was too big and the Lord too small. Our solution for helping people centred around dealing with the darkness, trying to cast the demons out and heal life's hurts instead of receiving more of the Holy Spirit's presence and power as a main emphasis.

Seeking God

This feeling of frustrated helplessness was put into a totally different context in the autumn of 1992. At one of Benny Hinn's meetings at Toronto's Maple Leaf Gardens, John and Carol realised that as Christians we truly have a 'big God' who can heal thousands of men and women in a single night – and heal the wheelchair bound and dozens of seriously ill people too.

As a consequence, they 'purposed in our hearts that we must have more of the anointing, so we began to seek God in a fresh way'. So, in October 1992, they gave over their mornings entirely to God, spending time in worship, prayer, reading the Bible, and just luxuriating in his presence. The expression to 'seek God' is not a meaningless idiom, it has to do with a sincere attempt to establish deep fellowship and communion with God. They did this for eighteen months, and they 'fell in love with Jesus all over again'. In retrospect, it is clear that this decision was vital in the shaping of their lives for the momentous work ahead.

Permanently changed

Just over a year later they travelled with Ed Silvoso to Argentina where revival had broken out in 1984 under the leadership of Carlos Annacondia, a revival that has been described as a 'revival of holiness'. John and Carol visited a maximum security prison in La Plata, near Buenos Aires and were met with a wave of people singing in Spanish, 'I'm free.' As John later recounted, 'We came to bless them and they [the prisoners] prayed for us and we were all out on the floor in prison.' This was a truly memorable occasion for the Arnotts who were also touched by the hand-made gifts the prisoners gave them. They were also powerfully impacted by the preaching and personal example of Claudio Freidzon, an Assemblies of God pastor. Freidzon prayed for them and, according to John's own account, their lives were permanently changed. Carol was completely over-whelmed by the Holy Spirit's power, and she was laughing so much that she could not walk straight. John was affected too, receiving an impartation of faith for more of God's presence, love, power and miraculous healings.

Heightened expectations

Hardly surprisingly, they returned from Argentina with increased expectations that God would do something fresh in their church, a glimpse of which was noticed in the New Year's Eve service when many people, when prayed for, were touched by God's power and presence. At that time, however, John and Carol did not anticipate that this visitation from God would be sustained. That same month an invitation to Randy Clark was accepted. He agreed to minister at Toronto for four nights, and the rest is history.

Chapter Four

The Qualities

There is a fascinating dichotomy at the heart of the published material on the Toronto Blessing. On the one hand, it has been vigorously, even implacably, opposed by many people, and unrelenting criticism has emanated from almost all the major denominations with varying degrees of intensity. For example, in his consideration of 'The Roots of the Toronto Blessing', Peter Fenwick comments as follows: 'sanctification – love of God, love of the Scriptures etc. – is demonstrably biblical, whilst all other features of the Toronto Blessing are not. [The] testimonies are, in fact, being used to authenticate the Toronto Blessing as a whole, the argument being that if the Toronto Blessing results in sanctification, it must be of God and so therefore must its manifestations and methodology'.[51] A possibly more extreme reaction is found in an investigative report on *Holy Laughter and the Toronto Blessing*, published by Zondervan,[52] attributing the Blessing to demonic activity and to the work of the Antichrist 'to bring about world apostasy and the creation of one-world church under satanic delusion'.

The intention of quoting these viewpoints is simply to show the extent to which the Toronto Blessing has elicited very strong reactions, not all of which have contributed to a reasoned and polemical debate on the issue.

However, few if any of the most committed and virulent opponents of the Toronto Blessing have criticised John and Carol's motives and intentions, still less have they impugned

85

their characters. Several reasons may help to explain this fact. One is that they were not particularly well known outside Canada prior to the events of January 1994, having attracted little attention in either the Christian or the secular media. Another is that they tend to operate, though not exclusively, within the association known as 'Partners in Harvest' – that is, those churches and ministries in direct relationship with them. Also, few of the Blessing's proponents and supporters have written much about them in biographical terms. A final reason is that they themselves have not courted publicity, preferring instead to get on with the work God has called them to, preserving their anonymity behind their preaching and ministry.

So what are John and Carol like as people?

In general, those who have either known them closely or have worked with them in an associate capacity speak highly of them. David Campbell, for example, senior pastor at City Church in St Albans, England, refers to 'their capacity to show the loving acceptance and care that the Father has for each one of us. John and Carol are a naturally pastoral couple, and the Father's blessing has been so focused on releasing the intimacy and awe of the Father.'[53] Dr Mark Stibbe, vicar of St Andrew's Church, Chorleywood, refers to 'their generous hearts. They just love giving away what they have received.'[54] Stuart Bell, leader of the New Life Christian Fellowship, Lincoln, sensed in John and Carol 'a great compassion for those who are hurting',[55] while Paul Wakely describes John as 'an apostle of love. I never heard a whisper of pride in all the time I was with him.'[56]

These snapshots are useful as they represent the views of four respected and experienced British leaders. Guy Chevreau writes in *Catch The Fire* that he has the 'highest regard' for the Arnotts, considering them to be 'some of the most gracious, generous and humble people I know.' In the same book, he adds that John and Carol have an unquenchable desire for the Holy Spirit and his work in the church today; and also that they are receptive to the perceptions of others who value 'the presence and power of God in their ministries.'

Another person who knows them well is Dave Markee, senior pastor (with his wife Ze) of Folly's End Church, a flourishing charismatic church in Croydon, South London. He says

> I was inspired by John and Carol to enjoy the Holy Spirit, the presence of God, because they love to see God at work building his kingdom. They are gentle and genuine people who welcome the Holy Spirit with no boundaries or restrictions. They always want more of God; and the more they get the more they want. The Holy Spirit found in John and Carol willing persons to allow the Holy Spirit to have his way, and crucially to follow his directions. Both are determined to trust God in each and every circumstance.

Colin Dye too, senior pastor at Kensington Temple, has formed clear and definite impressions about them: 'They are affirming, patient and loving people in whose lives the fruit of the Holy Spirit is abundantly present. Being with them as people, and also ministering with them, helped to make me more hungry for God.'

One final snapshot is provided by Dr R.T. Kendall, formerly senior pastor at Westminster Chapel for many years. Recalling John Arnott's visit to the chapel, he says: 'People stood in every second pew and he prayed for them; great blessing followed. He preached twice that day and the people fell in love with him. His Canadian manner and gentle demeanor endeared him to our congregation and helped them appreciate the authenticity of what was happening; his sermons helped people to see how biblical his preaching was.'[57]

The viewpoints presented by Colin Dye and R.T. Kendall illustrate a fundamental point. Their churches have never had any formal affiliation to the Toronto Blessing or 'Partners in Harvest', but they were able to identify qualities of character and demeanour in John and Carol that they found impressive and winsome: the fruit of the Holy Spirit in their everyday lives and ministries.

As preparation for this book many people who had had contact with the Arnotts were interviewed, and all were asked the same question: 'What are they like as people?' The striking fact was that all of them, albeit in different ways and to varying degrees of emphasis, pointed to the same characteristics.

1. PASSION

The word 'passion' here means to be 'stirred up, warm-blooded and awakened to the things of God' (Frank Damazio).[58] A desire for God, his presence and his requirements is present in both Old and New Testaments. The psalms, for example, contain many references to 'yearning', 'longing', even 'panting' for God. Another important word in this context is 'to thirst', the implication being that only God can really satisfy the longings and desires of the human heart. An appropriate example in the New Testament is Paul's 'For to me, to live is Christ and to die is gain' (Phil. 1:21, NIV). As Frank Damazio rightly comments: 'Jesus, who is our ultimate model, was a man of passion. He had a passion to fulfil the redemptive work that God had set before Him, to build His church and to defeat the gates of hell. He had a passion for people, a passion for the harvest.'[59]

Revival history confirms that a passion for God leads to an acute realisation of his presence. It is not possible for a person to *know* God without his/her feelings being involved. Dr Martyn Lloyd-Jones made this point slightly differently: 'The immediate effect [of God being among his people] is that the people present begin to have an awareness of spiritual things and clear views of them such as they have never had before.'[60] And Duncan Campbell, the human face of the Hebridean Revival 1949–52, says that its outstanding characteristic was the 'felt presence of God'.[61] Revival history also confirms that men and women who have a passion for God, during a remarkable move of God's Spirit, find that their passion is increased and heightened.

It is not hyperbole to talk about John and Carol Arnott in the context of passion for God. While some commentators have mocked the expression 'more Lord', it does nevertheless characterise their longing for more of God's presence in their lives, in a way that leads to obedience to him. As Dr J. Hudson Taylor said, in Duncan Campbell's hearing, 'God gives His

Holy Spirit not [just] to those who long for Him, not [just] to those who pray for Him, not [just] to those who desire to be filled always; He gives His Spirit to those who obey.'[62] John and Carol have a defined sense of the majesty of God and especially of the salvation made possible through Jesus Christ alone (Acts 4:12). And the outbreak of the Toronto Blessing has not slaked or satisfied their passion for God: it has increased it, and they continually relate it to the New Testament teaching on holiness and godly separation from the standards of the world. In their preaching, they stress the imperative of passion for God leading to a changed way of life, an awe of God that should change and sanctify the way men and women live; and in these matters they point to the need for knowledge of, and obedience to, the word of God. Their experience of God, both before and after January 1994, has led them to emphasise the need for a love of the Father, for the Scriptures, and for a desire to be free of besetting sins, which is and always has been the route to freedom for Christian people.

2. HUMILITY

John and Carol were genuinely amazed by the events starting on 20 January 1994, for at least two reasons. One was that they had never imagined that God would call *them* to lead an important work of God. Another was that on previous occasions when God had moved powerfully, it had only been for a limited and finite period of time. As John himself explained in an article for *Spread the Fire* (February 1999), 'When 1994 came we were plugging along, doing our best to be faithful to God's call upon our lives. Our 6-year old church had grown nicely to about 360 people, Jeremy Sinnott and I were fairly content that things were growing, yet I was well aware that we were a long way from affecting our city and nation. There was a deep cry in my heart, "God give us more". Carol and I were in the midst of a renewed season of seeking the face of God every morning . . . [and] God had deposited a longing in my heart to see His power over all the years that we had been holding our summer family camps. It seemed that the River of God would begin flowing for the two weeks of camp and then stop. Things would return to "normal" where nothing much happened. I longed for the momentum of summer camps to continue.'

John's words show his humble acceptance of what was happening in his church at that time, his sense of frustration, but his consummate desire for a work of God that would continue. There is no suggestion here that he would be called to lead a work of greater importance than what was then Toronto Airport Vineyard church, though when the call came both John and Carol felt 'honoured' by God's choice.

Humility is a highly prized virtue in the Bible, and the psalmist (Ps. 34:2) declares that the 'humble shall hear thereof and be glad' (KJV), while the writer of Proverbs 16:19 counsels that it is 'better to be of an humble spirit with the lowly, than to divide the spoil with the proud' (KJV). In the Old Testament there is a specific blessing attached to the whole concept of humility (and prayer): 'if my people, who are called by my name, will humble themselves and pray and seek my face and turn from their wicked ways, then I will hear from heaven and will forgive their sin and will heal their land' (2 Chr. 7:14, NIV). The supreme example, of course, is our Lord who humbled himself and became obedient even to death on the cross (see Phil. 2:8). It is also pertinent to recall the words of Jonathan Edwards who links the concepts of love and humility like this

> The surest character of true divine supernatural love, distin-guishing it from counterfeits that do arise from a natural self-love, is that Christian virtue shines in it, that does above all others renounce and abase and annihilate self, viz humility. Christian love, or true charity, is a humble love. When therefore we see love in persons attended with a sense of their own littleness, vileness, weakness, and utter insufficiency; and do so with self-diffidence, self-emptiness, self-renunciation, and a poverty of spirit, these are the manifest tokens of the Spirit of God (See End Notes:10).

John and Carol fully appreciate that the kingdom of God is not a matter of self-aggrandisement or self-glorification – their hearts says Ken Gott, a well-known preacher in north-east England, 'are only for the kingdom of God'.[63] Indeed the Toronto outpouring has been described earlier in this book by one of the Arnotts' associates as a 'revival of nobodies from nowhere', a view the Arnotts readily accept because they recognise that it certainly did not happen because of them or their ministry. This humility demonstrates itself in their lifestyle and when travelling. No special demands are made, there is no expectation of first-class travel or five-star hotel accommodation. So no special treatment is required, and certainly no attempt is made to impress people; and this unpretentious and unassuming approach is allied to a control and a gentleness that impresses those they come into contact with. In this sense too, they are modelling ministry lifestyle for their staff at TACF: the only hero, they frequently assert in their preaching, is Jesus.

3. PASTORAL HEARTS

From the start of their ministry in Stratford they have reached out to the divorced, the hurting, the sad, the lonely and the broken. Being divorced themselves John and Carol have a ready empathy for those going through similarly distressing times, not least to pastors who have travelled to Toronto on the verge of leaving the ministry. Not all have been refreshed, but many hundreds have found their love for Jesus, their congregations and the ministry reignited. The Reverend Malcolm Round, a Scottish Anglican pastor, records (*Spread the Fire*, February 1999) that since his first visit to Toronto in 1994 his life has been radically changed: 'This beaten up, burned out, ready-to-quit minister has fallen in love with Jesus again, rediscovered the Father's heart and the Holy Spirit's presence. I began to love the Word (of God) again and rediscovered the joy of worship.'

John and Carol are able to reach out instinctively to those in pain and anguish, and Ian and Janice Ross recall vividly their kindness and caring attitudes when the Ross family were undergoing problems with the health of one of their daughters. At that time, they felt that the Arnotts were being a spiritual 'mother' and 'father' to them, something they much appreci-ated. Here again they were modelling the ministry to those on their staff, not artificially but as warm-hearted, pastorally-inclined people.

Their pastoral 'feel' for men and women has its root in an intense awareness of God's love and the need to express that realisation in human and humane ways. This passion is intimately linked to their willingness to listen to God and to remain humble and teachable themselves. Dr Mark Stibbe has written, in *Experience The Blessing*: 'What I see in Toronto is an astonishing outpouring of the Father's love, driving out fear and breaking off chains. It has truly been a place where orphans have become heirs and slaves have become sons.'[64] In this sense, what happens at Toronto is also a reflection of the hearts of John and Carol who are keenly aware that it is all to be attributed to God's wonderful grace and compassion.

4. VISION

This quality is mentioned primarily in relation to John Arnott. Those who have worked with him, both in Stratford and in Toronto, draw attention to the fact that he is constantly producing new ideas and fresh initiatives, though sometimes, as his staff say with a rueful grin, he goes ahead of them without fully thinking of the administrative complexities and difficulties.

Never content with the status quo, the comfortable or the routine, he is always wanting to press ahead with ideas that may be two or three years down the line. This makes TACF an exciting, if exhausting, place to be. Some of the fruits of his vision include the various Schools of Ministry (five-month long) and Leadership (one-month long) courses and also what is known as the 'Soaking Prayer' initiative, which encourages men and women to spend time listening to God's voice and praying to him. The rationale behind this initiative is explained by John as follows

> In the beginning God created man and woman. His greatest joy was the close fellowship (or communion) he had with them as they walked and talked together in the garden, enjoying the cool of the day. But it didn't last. Satan brought sin into the world and broke that precious, intimate relationship. So man began to search for something to fill the emptiness in his heart. Thank God Jesus came and restored mankind into relationship with the Father. Now the

Holy Spirit comes to soften our hearts, re-kindle our love for our heavenly dad and make us ready for a new love relationship. Soaking prayer is simply us coming to be with our Father, no shopping lists, no agendas, just ourselves being still in his arms of love.

Thousands of people, in forty-two countries throughout the world have committed themselves to this idea, with enormous personal and spiritual and emotional benefits. Overarching the whole initiative is John's desire that pockets of renewal and revival will break out in all the continents of the world.

Frequently too, pastors have gone away from Toronto with a vision of their own. An example of this is the ministry of Willi Stewart, an Anglican minister who leads a congregation called CORE (City Outreach through Renewal and Evangelism) in Dublin. It was in Toronto that he was given a vision to start a church that would reach out effectively into Ireland and the city of Dublin in particular. Through C.O.R.E. he has been able to reach people who would otherwise remain for ever untouched by the normal procedures of church growth.[65]

5. 'REALNESS'
Linguistically there is no such word as 'realness', so 'reality' would be a more appropriate word. It implies an acceptance of life as it is, not as it is supposed to be or how men and women would like it to be. It is the very opposite of pretence, and involves an honest perspective, together with an emotional control and calmness.

John's emotional control was put under extreme testing when the then TAV was effectively expelled from the Vineyard Association. Both John and Carol were deeply impressed with John Wimber's approach to ministry, particularly his desire to empower every Christian for ministry, and soon after establishing their first church in Stratford they began an informal relationship with the Vineyard churches. Wimber was a 'father figure' to the Arnotts, and Carol felt 'devastated' by the decision – it felt like a family break-up to her, with a sundering of valued and close links fostered over a significant number of years.

At the meeting itself John understood that the decision to expel his church was irrevocable, non-negotiable, and he accepted it calmly. In fact, one of his staff members said that 'John Arnott was the calmest person in the room'. It's not that he was devoid of feelings, and he shared Jeremy Sinnott's feeling of 'fatherlessness'. He also felt frustration at the thought of being disciplined without the reasons being fully explained, and no opportunity for discussion offered. But he was determined to carry on with God's work in Toronto and around the world: he was determined to persevere, that it should be 'business as usual'. Ever the visionary, John Arnott looked to the future at a deeply upsetting time: 'Now we can give renewal to churches around the world' – which is what has transpired.

6. INTEGRITY

Integrity is vitally important to John and Carol. John constantly emphasises integrity and accountability in the running of the church in Toronto. Nowhere is this more apparent than in the financial rectitude with which TACF is organised. As one of the associate pastors said, 'John Arnott is not in the ministry for the money.' He is in it to fulfil God's plans and to exhibit the fruit of the Spirit in discharging his many and varied duties. Both John and Carol are transparent in this respect, and demand the highest standards from their fellow workers . . . as they do of themselves.

This matter of integrity was something John learned in the 1960s when, as a young Christian, he attended the Queensway Cathedral. His pastor at that time was Alex Ness, and he gave John sage and valuable advice: 'If you are serious about going into the ministry, watch out for three things: women, money and issues of power and control.' Others have called these snares 'the girls, the gold and the glory'. They are really pertinent because so many times famous and successful servants of God have been brought down by one of these temptations. When this happens, of course, reproach and pain is caused to the body of Christ. John places a very high value on what has taken place in Toronto, commenting as follows: 'This anointed renewal is a holy and breathtaking gift from

God. In order for the Holy Spirit to remain with us, we need to place a great value on his manifest presence. We need to be protective of the Father's Blessing, living holy lives and keeping our eyes on Jesus.' John and Carol desire with all their hearts to be 'faithful stewards' of God's anointing; and they are clear that to continue to enjoy the anointing they must remain teachable and humble, and not to become 'loose cannons' who damage God's kingdom. They are also adamant that God's anointing must not, at all costs, be used to gain wealth or personal glory or credibility for themselves.

7. 'UNRELIGIOUS'
Neither John nor Carol is interested in hype or frothy excitement, nor are they interested in revivalism or renewalism. It has to be of and from the Holy Spirit or they don't want it. They are constantly learning from God, constantly reading, especially of God's ways in great move- ments of the past. Their attitude is reminiscent of John Angell James' comment in *When God Moves*, by John Armstrong, 'I do not desire, I do not advise bustling, artificial efforts to get up a revival, nor the construction of any man-devised machinery. I want God's work, not man's. I want no revivalist preachers.'[66]

The seven qualities of character listed and briefly explored above are, in general, the work of God's grace and shaping in their lives over many years before 1994. They built levels of character into their lives in obscurity, including the fact 'that God hates sin' (Jonathan Edwards). They didn't suddenly become holy or pious as a result of the Toronto Blessing, they had always appreciated the need for lives that please God. However, before someone jumps (wrongly) to the conclusion that this book is implying that they are flawless, an obvious remark needs to be made: John and Carol Arnott are as fallible as anyone else! They make mistakes, sometimes fail to give correct information, lose their sense of balance, and can be unreasonable. John gets as disappointed as the next person when someone has let him down. All pretty normal, but the fact remains that, in the unanimous verdict of those who know them well, John and Carol have a genuineness that leads people to trust them. As Ken Gott has said, 'God has given us the security of knowing we can trust our lives to them.' No praise could be higher.

Explanation

The above qualities, however, didn't simply arrive one day by carrier pigeon or the Canadian equivalent of Parcel Force in Britain. What then explains the rise and development of these qualities? In response, it is possible to identify a number of key factors.

First, John and Carol place a high value on the teaching of the Bible, with its clear emphasis on the need for genuineness of life and behaviour. It is perhaps a cliché to say that men and women of God are the same in private as they are in public, but it is true of them, as many of their fellow-workers have testified. Leaders of revival are not primarily of importance because they shake or fall down; rather it is because they exhibit a quality of character and approach that exalts the Lord Jesus, which again can be said of the Arnotts.

Second, they have a clear understanding of salvation and faith. They constantly reiterate the need for salvation to be 'worked out' in daily life, in a practical and demonstrable sense. They view faith, perfectly appropriately, as the fundamental, totally indispensable building block of our Christian lives. As John wrote in *Revolutionizing Faith* (published in 2002 by Sovereign World), 'The whole of the Christian life is about faith that works by love'; and he argues, in the same book, that faith has nothing to do with either a person's faith in their faith or in their abilities – rather it is about being childlike before God, 'putting our trust in Him and then resting in that, expecting Him to do all that He has promised to do and living in hope, because that is what God has called us to.'

Third, both are the products of brokenness. Frank Damazio pertinently comments as follows: 'Anything that is broken is deemed by man to be unfit, and he ends up throwing it away. But to God, only that which is broken is useful ... So the vessels of God are ready for revival only when they are broken. God's vessels, the ones He uses, are broken vessels.'[67] Both John and Carol were devastated by the experience of divorce from their first partners, and John felt that he would never trust a woman again, so much so that when he asked Carol to marry him, he was amazed when she said 'yes' immediately. She helped him to rebuild his life. Their painful experience with their first partners dealt with something in their hearts, stripping them of pride and self-confidence, and thus ready for the infilling of the Holy Spirit.

Fourth, and it follows from the above paragraph, a rock-solid marriage is a vitally important factor when discussing their qualities. Carol reignited in John the willingness to trust another woman again, while he encouraged her to minister in a way she would never have imagined previously. She frequently says that she couldn't sing (and still can't, according to her friends!), couldn't play the piano, had no experience of preaching, and was thus an unlikely candidate to be a pastor's wife. But that's what she has become, and she attributes this to the gentle leading and guiding of her husband. To see them working together is an instructive model for Christian leaders in general, as far too often in the western World the woman is an adjunct to the man in ministry, thus depriving congregations of at least 50 per cent of the wisdom. John and Carol are effective because they operate out of a relationship which is devoid of striving or competitiveness, and is all the stronger as a consequence.

Fifth, they are keen to obey the promptings of the Holy Spirit in all aspects of their ministry together. Colleagues constantly refer to their love of the work and presence of the Holy Spirit. Once convinced that they should pursue a particular pathway, they go after it tenaciously. This openness to the Holy Spirit has also enabled them to maintain, in Jack Taylor's words, 'faithfulness, authenticity and perseverance'.

Sixth, they maintain a disciplined lifestyle of reading the Scriptures and prayer. Before the outbreak of the Toronto Blessing they devoted their mornings for the previous eighteen months to worship, prayer and studying the Bible together; and it is something to adhere to when not travelling.

Seventh, they take absolutely seriously the question of forgiveness. This is apparent in John's little booklet published by Sovereign World in 1997, *Forgiveness: Biblical Truths Simply Explained*, which has sold hundreds of thousands of copies. They frequently refer to Isaiah 61:1 – the Lord has come to set captives free and to open prison doors – in the context of the freedom and healing that comes when forgiveness is given a free rein. Nothing, in their view, is as gloriously liberating or as releasing. Again it is important to stress that this teaching is closely related to their life experiences. As John says, 'When my first marriage broke up, I made a vow that no woman would ever hurt me like that again. It took me quite a while, with Carol's help, to break down that vow. I thank God that Carol penetrated my defences. It meant that I was able to be healed of judgements rooted in bitterness, and to see mercy triumphing over judgement.'

Eighth, the cultivation of core values, which are aptly summed up by the acronym FIRE.

F refers to the Father's Love, I has to do with the Intimacy we can all enjoy with the Father, R refers to the Restoration of the heart, while E has to do with the Equipping of the Holy Spirit for life and ministry. These core values are central to the teaching of TACF and to the various schools of Ministry and Leadership there.

Ninth, they often refer to the question of accountability. At all levels of leadership men and women are made aware of their accountability to God, in the first instance, then to the church and to each other. John and Carol hold themselves accountable to the other leaders and, crucially, are open to advice and comments from others.

Tenth, they love people, and the congregation and workers at TACF miss them hugely when they are travelling. Although different in terms of temperament – Carol is as warmly outgoing as John is phlegmatic and less demonstrative – they both clearly enjoy being with other people, and John in particular has a keen, often sharp, sense of humour.

Overview

John and Carol have affected thousands of men and women around the world. This is due, in no small measure, to their ability to transcend denomination, culture and differing lifestyles. They are as at home in the deprived circumstances of the Ukraine and Mozambique as they are in the more affluent, though no less needy, western world of Canada, America and Britain. They are constantly reaching out to the hurting and the angst-ridden, and their naturalness is something that is deeply impressive. So too is the ordinariness and humility of their travelling requirements: not for them five-star luxury or permanent first-class travel. No exorbitant financial demands either. Much more important to them is the loving and honouring of other people, retaining, as one British leader (Paul Wakely) put it in *By Their Fruits*, 'the right kind of authority, within which, there was immense freedom and huge encouragement to respond to God'. No praise could be higher exemplifying, as it does, qualities of character rather than charisma.

Chapter Five

The Significance

Over ten years have elapsed since the dramatic and momentous events of January 1994 and the spread of the Toronto Blessing to many countries of the world. As suggested earlier, it has been subjected to enormous scrutiny from a number of different perspectives: personal, sociological, denominational and theological. This has been done in an attempt to identify its essential nature and significance, with such questions as 'Is it biblical?' or 'Is it revival?' at the nerve centre of the discussion. An indication of its effect may be deduced from the fact that the file on the Toronto Blessing in the Evangelical Alliance archive alone is at least six inches thick. In addition, scores of books – both in North America and Britain – have been written about it, many of them admittedly in the immediate aftermath of January 1994.

Contrasting viewpoints abound, often from within the same denominational parameters, which suggests that the question 'What is the Toronto Blessing about?' remains tantalising and fascinating. The purpose of this chapter is to summarise briefly a number of the main interpretations offered and to place the ministry of John and Carol Arnott in the context of the Toronto Blessing as a whole. After all, they have led and inspired its development since its inception and so their views are important. Their amazement at what has happened is as genuine and as deeply rooted now as it was originally, and they continue to lead TACF with a defined sense of enjoyment and purpose. Eventually, as John will reach retiring age in December 2005, consideration will need to be given to their successor or successors, but at the moment they are utterly contented with their roles, even though it involves criss-crossing the world in a daunting and exhausting schedule of meetings and travelling. To some, frequent travel to a variety of different locations might appear to be glamorous or even romantic, but they are always keen to return to the leadership of the TACF where they are greatly missed when absent from the day-to-day rounds of activities.

Like it or not, the Toronto Blessing is a fixed point in the history of the church, though clearly it is not possible or advisable to pronounce on its final place in the history of Christianity. Some entertained hopes that it would lead to a global revival in preparation for the Second Coming, though manifestly worldwide revival has yet to occur, but which millions throughout the world continue to pray for. On the other hand, some commentators have already pronounced the death of the Toronto Blessing. One such person is Rob Warner:[68] 'Toronto came in with a bang but, frankly, ended with a whimper.' He does though characterise it as a 'time of deep spiritual enrichment and rekindled hope for revival'. He also saw it as a time of being turned off by 'exaggeration, manipulation and hysteria', concluding that 'Perhaps Toronto is best seen as a parable of the mixed brew that is revival.' Clive Calver,[69] formerly Director General of the Evangelical Alliance, concurs with this perspective, commenting like this: 'You have never had an awakening [defined as that which God does when he turns society around] in history that hasn't started in renewal and revival.'

Changes at TACF

With these brief initial comments as a starting-point, it is important to consider the significance of the Toronto Blessing in slightly more detail, starting with TACF whose members were as surprised as John and Carol with the events at the start of 1994.

At the end of 1993 membership was approximately four hundred, but soon people began to arrive, first in their hundreds, then soon in their thousands. A previously settled and regular routine was about to be disrupted in a fairly spectacular fashion. Big conference events such as 'Catch The Fire' (almost six thousand people attended the first one held at the Regal Constellation Hotel), 'The Father Loves You', and 'The Party Is Here' (also known by the title 'Let The River Flow') were perceived, quite wrongly, by some of the members to dwarf the daily and ongoing work of the church, thus causing tension, and some did leave. The tension was made worse by the decision to abandon pastoral (or cell) groups, numbering seven in all, in favour of attendance at the nightly meetings. The consequence of this decision was that the number of adults in the church fell to a hundred. They probably left because of the need for connectedness and meaningful relationships, but the situation, in terms of the local church, was later rectified when the cell structure was reintroduced. Today there are 165 cell groups based on a refined form of the Government of 12 Structure. All these groups are pastoral, but are also concerned with the growing and equipping of leaders. Importantly, leaders at TACF are chosen not on their gifts alone, but also on their characters. Membership has increased ten-fold since 1994, although Toronto, in common with other major cities, probably has a complete change of membership every six years, reflecting the reality of city life in Canada.

Administrative changes followed too, especially the need for increased staff and volunteers, all of course requiring additional financial resources, not to mention the need for a new building: Dixie Road was far too small to accommodate the visitors regularly arriving from all over the world, as well as being noisy due to its close proximity to a huge international airport. Increased pastoral help was needed too with the organisation of the weekly schedule of meetings: prayer counsellors, worship teams and preachers. Such a burden could not possibly be sustained by the resources at TACF alone, and hundreds of men and women from other churches in Toronto and the surroundings towns offered their help and assistance sacrificially.

By March/April 1994 attendance at the nightly meetings was conservatively estimated at a thousand, a 50 per cent increase in four months. Significant numbers of people began to arrive from North America, with a limited number, estimated at approximately thirty each week, coming from Britain too. By September 1994, 30,000 people had visited the church. What was a trickle initially became a wave, then a torrent, and to this day thousands attend the major conferences at TACF. The tenth and eleventh 'Catch The Fire' conferences were attended by 4,000 people each. In the 2004 conference, for example, there were visitors from approximately forty countries, with hundreds coming for the first time.

The weekly meetings have remained largely unvaried. On Monday there is no meeting, then from Tuesday to Saturday there are renewal meetings, followed by two services on Sunday. The meetings themselves have also followed a broadly similar pattern, consisting of worship, testimonies, preaching, and then prayer ministry. This pattern of meetings reflects John and Carol's core values and emphases in their ministry.

Changes in John and Carol's lifestyle

But if January affected the life of TACF, how much more was this true of the Arnotts. Previously the pastors of a rather obscure church with not even a national profile in Canada, they became 'famous', being exposed at least in the early years to relentless media exposure. This was not something they wanted, but they saw it as something inevitably linked to what was occurring in their church. International travel was now part and parcel of their lives, together with an unrelenting programme of meetings, which often meant that they were unable to spend as much time in prayer as they would like. Their innate humility, however, safeguarded them from the pride and self-importance that sometimes accompanies what is perceived of as a jet-set life: actually anyone acquainted with the vagaries of flying knows that it is simply tiring and often frustrating. People did though clamour for their opinion, and for visits to their churches and conferences. Nowadays John and Carol limit their travelling to a hundred days a year, and nothing gives them greater pleasure than returning to their home and to their church family at TACF.

Of one thing there is no doubt, their lives were radically changed by the outpouring of the Holy Spirit in January 1994, for which they are immensely grateful.

Controversy

The Toronto Blessing, however, has a much greater significance than merely the local dimensions of the Arnotts lives and the marked changes in their church. It undoubtedly had – and has – an international dimension, the first being the controversy it aroused. Everyone, it seems, had an opinion to express, not least those who had sharply critical verdicts to promulgate. People, who from the outset, were implacably opposed or whose initial enthusiasm declined, tended to see the Blessing in primarily negative terms, while others were distinctly hostile to the point of being abusive. So it was interpreted as:

- Group hysteria
- Psychological manipulation
- Psychological violence
- Public humiliation
- Demonic distraction.

The argument, as far as the first two interpretations above are concerned, is that it was the result of auto-suggestion or emotionalism, on the one hand, or that it was somehow engineered by leaders so that their own ministries were bolstered. The Dean of Worcester, Robert Jeffrey, denounced the Toronto Blessing (in *'Toronto' in Perspective*) 'as an expression of hysteria which could lead to a ghetto mentality, and the undermining of an intellectually respectable faith'. Seldom are such blanket statements helpful, and the views of Martin Davie[70] are more pertinent. He points out that the diverse ways in which the Blessing affected people, and the way it spread in so many different countries, makes it extremely difficult to accept the view that it was auto-suggestion. In fact, such an approach would require more faith than to see it as a genuine act of God. Davie also propounds the valid argument that even allowing for the involvement of psychological and/or sociological factors would not rule out God's activity. The auto-suggestion argument also founders on the genuineness, uncomplicated and un-manipulative approaches of John and Carol Arnott.

The third criticism was put forward by David Pawson, who asserts that the phenomena associated with the Toronto Blessing are to be viewed as public and embarrassing humiliation of the men and women concerned, commenting: 'Certainly we need to be humbled, though most exhortations in Scripture are to humble ourselves. There is, however, a fine though important distinction between being humbled and being humiliated. The latter carries overtones of being degraded and despised. No wise parent humiliates a child, knowing what can damage can result. Would the heavenly Father do otherwise?'[71] Not one of the hundreds of people the author has spoken to perceive it in this way; and the same people drew attention to the new intimacy they found in their relationship with God.

The demonic distraction theory was prominent in the criticisms of Alan Morrison, who describes the phenomena as 'the outworking of a childish and hysterical mimicry; at worst, they are the result of something far more sinister' (quoted in *'Toronto' in Perspective*). Presumably the latter phrase implies that the Toronto Blessing is to be perceived as the work of Satan, and certainly this was the view of Dr David Jenkins, formerly Bishop of Durham: 'it is a form of manipulation which reinforces the superstitious side of religion'; and he added: '[It is] increasingly clear [that] this cannot be the work of the Holy Spirit, who is the vehicle of God in Jesus who loves us and treats us with respect.' (quoted in *'Toronto' in Perspective*) Against these views may be placed the series of questions posed by the late (and hugely respected) Dr Martyn Lloyd-Jones: 'Why should the Devil suddenly start doing this kind of thing? Here is the church in a period of dryness and drought; why should the Devil suddenly do something which draws attention to religion and Jesus Christ?' When he spoke these words (in a series of sermons originally preached in 1959) Dr Lloyd-Jones was not, of course, talking about the Toronto Blessing, but his argument is surely applicable in a general sense.

John and Carol have never sought to defend themselves against the criticisms. They do not, in the first instance, have the time, being fully occupied with their ministry in Toronto and around the world; and they are content to point to the fruit in people's lives. But what sort of fruit?

A Defined Sense of God's Presence

The presence and power of God were evident in early revivals in North America. The sense of God's presence involves a sharp awareness of

- God's power and character
- The reality of spiritual matters
- The sheer futility of worldly issues

and leads to an increased understanding of the Holy Spirit's work and influence. An intense awareness of God's presence was a feature of the Welsh Revival 1904–05 too, and led to 'an intense hunger for the Word [of God], and the awakened ones could not tolerate anything but the Word, and that too spoken by those who had personal experience of its power in their own hearts and lives. It was to many almost a re-discovery of the old Book. And now people read it for practical purposes.'[72]

Those who have either visited Toronto or who have been in Toronto-style meetings have commented on a similarly powerful awareness of God's presence, an awareness heightened by the worship there with its concentration on the work of the cross, the Person of Jesus, and the love of the Father. John and Carol love the presence of God, nothing gives them greater pleasure and joy, and they seek to communicate these feelings wherever they go in the world. It is something that has characterised their ministry from the very start. In their meetings a sense of God is all-pervasive, and thousands of people have been converted in them. To be aware of God in a powerful way is one of the greatest blessings of the Christian life, and men and women who have been to Toronto 'carry' it with them, as Terry Moore reports after a visit to TACF. 'Instead of giving a report on our trip [to Toronto] we wanted to simply invite the Holy Spirit to come among us and then pray for the people in our church. We started praying about noon, and God began to move. As He did, our congregation responded in various ways. Some were weeping, others were laughing, and others were simply in awe of His presence.'[73] This testimony is reminiscent of the 'awe' that is referred to in the Acts of the Apostles when God's wonder and power were demonstrably evident. In God's presence at Toronto thousands of men and women have had life-changing experiences of his magnificent love and care for them. In this sense, it's not so much a theological understanding of his love but a felt experience. John and Paula Sandford, having similarly experienced the love of God, say this: 'We are now much more in love with Jesus than ever before. His presence saturates us with God's love every day. He refreshes and revitalises our walk in Him as often as we turn to Him.'[74] The Sandfords words are a most useful introduction to another crucial aspect of the Toronto Blessing's significance.

Refreshment

Many, many people, including pastors, have journeyed to Toronto in an exhausted, disillusioned or apathetic frame of mind. Church life had become tedious and repetitive and, crucially, devoid of power. There could be a number of reasons for this state, with excessive work or failure or immorality or divorce coming readily to mind. Whatever the reasons or causes, Toronto has been a place of refreshment and recovery. Marriages on the point of total dislocation have been put back together, an effusion of joy and renewed intimacy being the outcome. In a safe environment, people have rediscovered the mightiness and accessibility of God who loves everyone with an overwhelming love.

One such person in need of refreshment was a middle-aged pastor from mid-west America. Bill (not his real name) was burned out with the demands of a big church of almost a thousand members, but grimly determined to do everything himself, and desperately afraid to be 'honest' with his congregation in case they rejected him. A gifted and able man, he had a great deal of head knowledge but was suspicious of the workings of the Holy Spirit: he certainly did not wish to speak in tongues, and as far as prophecy was concerned, he was deeply suspicious, viewing it as an exaggerated form of guessing or, at worst, manipulation. Nor was his marriage successful either. His wife was withdrawn and 'closed down' to the point of being secretive, even reclusive. She had few friends in the church, her social life was extremely limited and, frankly, she found her husband's preaching boring and unproductive because of the tangible gap that divided the man in the pulpit and the man at home. Their teenagers had as much interest in church activities as a visitor from outer space might have. This was a family on the verge of total disintegration. To his wife's amazement, Bill suggested that they should visit Toronto where 'something unusual' was happening. To his surprise, she agreed: at least the food and shopping in Toronto would be good, and there was always the CN Tower to see.

Their general air of disenchantment and lethargy was not improved by their first visit to TACF. Frankly, in Bill's view, the preaching was ordinary, the worship raucous (a fact made worse by the guitarist with a back-to-front baseball cap perched precariously on his head), and some of the people were laughing uncontrollably. This was most decidedly not church, at least according to Bill, though his wife found it 'different' and 'lively'.

At the conclusion of the service, Bill's wife went back to the hotel, but he somewhat reluctantly stayed behind for prayer ministry. He waited rather a long time but eventually a small, white-haired woman came to pray for him. She mumbled a short prayer: 'Lord, please heal this man's inner anguish and sense of failure, and please make him a man of God in his own family.' Bill was outraged, wondering how she had known about him, which of course she didn't. At that point the power

of the Holy Spirit came irresistibly upon him and he fell
backwards, and rested peacefully on the floor.
Let Bill continue his story.

As I lay there, I heard God speak to me in ways I hadn't heard for
years. He spoke to me as a Father would speak to a son, assuring
me of his love and desires for me. In fresh and beautiful ways, God
began to restore me to his heart of love. I felt as if I was being
rocked in his arms like a child. God also showed me that I had
neglected my wife and family for the sake of my ministry, my
teaching, my gifts, and I understood that I was responsible, as a
Father, for my wife's backsliding and my children's rebellion: I
had not loved them as a husband and father should. He also
promised that he would restore my public ministry to fruitfulness
if only I obeyed him. I couldn't believe that he had used that little
old lady to speak to me so directly and so dynamically.

But he had. The upshot was that Bill eventually hurried back to
the hotel to ask his wife's forgiveness and, later, his children
too. Thus, as a family, they began a journey together as a
consequence of Bill's refreshment at Toronto. The key thing in
this story is that Bill's faith pre-Toronto was more about
performance than passion, more about ritual than relationship,
more about routine than intimacy, more about works than
faith, and certainly more about programme than the presence
of God. Bill's life was changed for the better in Toronto, and he
learned once again to walk in God's love and to give it away
with a renewed sense of urgency and genuine passion for those
who do not have a meaningful relationship with Jesus Christ.
Significantly too their marriage was restored and
reinvigorated. John and Carol are thrilled by the refreshment
that Toronto has brought to so many people around the world.
It is a word they frequently use when preaching and teaching.

Renewal

This is another of their favourite words to characterise what
has – and is – happening in Toronto. There can be no doubt that

the Toronto Blessing has had a marked impact on thousands who were already Christians in 1994, with a deepening of their relationship with God, which even some of the sharpest critics of the Toronto Blessing concede. John and Carol use the word 'renewal' in the sense of reawakening or reinvigorating or imparting a freshness to that which already exists in a person's Christian life. Several aspects of this renewal may be referred to:

• Hunger for God's word. John and Carol have a deep thirst for the word of God and regulate their lives – and lifestyles – according to its teaching and admonitions. The subject-matter of their preaching starts with God, humankind's fall from grace, the salvation provided by Jesus' death on the cross (substitutionary atonement), and the need for an ongoing experience of God as guided by the Holy Spirit. They soak themselves in the Scriptures and contrary to some criticism, they do not form judgements on an experiential rather than a rational, Bible-centred basis. But they do attract the ire of critics by saying that, at times, our heads need to be offended so that God can get to our hearts. There are, after all, times when our rationalism, our intellects and reason have to be bypassed. And they do, quite rightly, emphasise the need for a 'felt experience' of God. Theology that remains a body of cold abstractions about God is unlikely to be fruitful in terms of behaviour and power.

• An increased love for Jesus, his church and his followers. On this aspect the Arnotts' teaching is emphatic: 'People will tell you that the most important thing in the kingdom of God is to get the lost saved . . . The most important things in the kingdom of God is to develop a loving relationship with the Lord, getting to know Emmanuel – God with us. Christ in you the hope of glory [Col.1:27]!'

• An increased love of worship, of obedience, of evangelism and also of abundant joy. Joy is a fruit of the Holy Spirit, so it is no surprise that John frequently emphasises that men and women who are filled with the Holy Spirit are full of joy. So John and Carol teach that the Holy Spirit and joy go together, complement each other naturally and supernaturally; and this joy as John comments is 'greater than the joy that comes with material abundance, new cars, pay rises or promotions.' It is also a joy witnessed so often at Toronto when husbands and wives have restored their marriages. Much of the above may be related in individual or corporate terms, but a further aspect of the Toronto Blessing's significance has to do with the Pensacola outpouring, which began on Father's Day, 18 June 1995.

Toronto and Pensacola

The events in Pensacola, and what led up to them, have been fully chronicled in *Feast Of Fire* by John Kilpatrick,[75] formerly senior pastor at Brownsville Assemblies of God Church. Millions of visitors, mainly from America but also from across the world, made their way to Brownsville, where the outpouring had its roots in the Assemblies of God and American southern revivalism. Personal repentance and fear of God were its most prominent features whereas Toronto, perhaps reflecting its Vineyard roots, has laid a greater stress on the love of the Father and the delights and benefits of intimacy with him. Though different in nature, both outpourings have this common factor: 'both pastoral couples were hungry for revival. John and Brenda Kilpatrick, grieving the loss of John's mother, were longing for a revival which would set their congregation and their own hearts on fire. John and Carol Arnott were longing for a greater visitation of power to spread the gospel.' (from Melinda Fish's article in *Spread the Fire*)

John Kilpatrick visited Toronto for the first time in October 1998 and said, 'Without Toronto there likely would not have been a Pensacola.' He said this because his wife, Brenda, had visited Toronto in February 1995 and had been powerfully touched by God, including being completely healed of back problems. On her return to Brownsville, she began to have an intimacy with the Lord that she never knew existed. This relationship was so deeply satisfying in her spirit that she returned to Brownsville with an energised determination to

pray for revival and within a few months (18 June 1995) everything changed at her church as well. On a personal level too
Brenda Kilpatrick's life has changed radically, with the timidity
that kept her away from crowds being replaced by enjoyment
at being able to share what God has done for her.

Toronto and Pensacola are entirely different in style and
emphasis, but both have been used by God to 'call in the
harvest and restore the church to a first-love passion for Jesus.
[They] are streams born of the same fresh river of blessing that
has sprung up in our day.'[76] There is a tempting analogy, which
Melinda Fish refers to in her article, that just as Wesley and
Whitefield were instruments in the same outpouring albeit
deploying different methods, so future church historians may
refer to Toronto and Brownsville as being twin instruments in
the same outpouring although again being different in their
styles and approaches. What is encouraging too is to observe
the two sets of leaders being mutually supportive while, at the
same time, recognising the differing methods employed.

Thus far, the significance of the Toronto Blessing has been
pursued from a number of different standpoints: changes at
TACF, radical alterations to the lifestyles of John and Carol,
especially vastly increased travelling and global leadership,
the reality of God's presence, refreshment and renewal, plus
the links and differences between the outpourings in Toronto
and Pensacola. Personal and collective dimensions have also
been referred to.

The assumption has been, quite unashamedly, that the
Toronto Blessing is a genuine move of God in which there has
been – and is – an increased love of God and other people. This
love emanates from an understanding of what John Armstrong
rightly calls 'the profound riches of God's free and sovereign
grace given to us in Christ alone', about which Jonathan
Edwards wrote (as already noted in Chapter Four)

> The surest character of true divine supernatural love,
> distinguishing it from counterfeits that do arise from a natural self-
> love, is that Christian virtue shines in it . . . Christian love, or true
> charity, is a humble love. When therefore we see love in persons
> attended with a sense of their own littleness, vileness, weakness

and utter insufficiency; and do so with self-diffidence, self-emptiness, self-renunciation, and a poverty of spirit, these are the manifest tokens of the Spirit of God.

It is in this context that the heart of John and Carol's ministry is to be located. Their overwhelming desire is to see passion for Jesus reignited, reformed and redirected so that the message of his sublime love can be taken to, and affect, the world. Neither John nor Carol is a conceptual thinker, and they are not primarily interested in ideas, but both have what one of their colleagues described as 'a burning desire to win people for Jesus; that's all they are concerned with.'

Unusual phenomena

Up to this point, no attempt has been made to discuss the significance of the Toronto Blessing in relation to unusual phenomena or manifestations. The reason for this could be that they do not represent its nerve centre and true significance. Physical manifestations are hardly a surprise when God is moving in power, with laughter and joy, falling down as though dead, trembling, groaning in the spirit, weeping, and being so drunk in the Spirit so as to be unable to walk. Opponents of the Blessing quickly depicted these phenomena, often intensely demonstrated, as sure evidence of fleshly behaviour by people courting attention out of their emotional, psychological or religious needs. Others, equally quickly, saw mental instability or the demonic at work; and even today many people disagree with the assertion that the phenomena do not represent the heart of the Toronto Blessing.

But there is ample justification for adopting the stance that no revival or great work of God however long or short its duration is to be interpreted primarily by its unusual events or phenomena, and from the very best of theological and pastoral sources too. The first of these is Jonathan Edwards, one of the greatest writers ever on the work of the Holy Spirit in revival. In his *Treatise on the Religious Affections*, he is scrupulous in his distinguishing what he dubs 'religious affections' from mere 'passions'; and he shows that 'affections' include the delight of the mind and the engagement of the will. So affections are not just emotions, and significantly he refuses to condemn or not place a high value on the emotional and the physical manifestations accompanying revival. What is Edwards' reasoning in this respect? In his view, they offer no conclusive proof, either negatively or positively, regarding the genuineness or authenticity of the experience.

In addition, Edwards lists many other things as offering no conclusive proof as to the authenticity of a work of God, including

- unusual bodily effects
- increased talk about the trivia of religious issues
- heightened imaginations
- unwise conduct
- irregular conduct
- errors of judgement
- satanic delusions
- heresy
- sinful behaviour
- excessive preaching about hell.

This is a comprehensive list that deserves to be considered with care and reflection.

The second source is the views of Dr Martyn Lloyd-Jones, not only one of the must astute writers on the whole subject of revival, but also a conservative evangelical, and most decidedly non-charismatic in his theology. In *Joy Unspeakable*,[77] he makes a number of telling points. One is that the phenomena, though not essential to revival, do tend to be present where there is revival; and he refers to fainting and falling to the ground, physical convulsions, states of unconsciousness or trances. And clearly he accepts the argument that the Holy Spirit affects the whole person, with body, soul and spirit being indivisible.

The evidence from both sources would suggest that for proponents and opponents to make too much of the phenomena witnessed at a time of divine visitation is, at best, unwise, and unfortunately the whole argument developed a furore that was not constructive: indeed perhaps such an approach is impossible with protagonists coming from different and often deeply entrenched standpoints. Blanket assertions, simplistic judgements, inaccurate reporting, and distortion of the Scriptures are not valid approaches, and this applies equally to both sides of the divide as far as the Toronto Blessing is concerned. Valuable lessons may be learned from Edwards and Lloyd-Jones, not least that there is no need to be afraid of an extraordinary and powerful movement of the Holy Spirit (Edwards); and that we should all desire the unction or anointing of the Spirit to attend the preaching of the word (Lloyd-Jones) so that preacher (and hearers) are equipped with boldness and authority to proclaim the gospel to those who desperately need it.

Regrettably initial reports on the TACF concentrated almost exclusively on the physical manifestations of the Spirit, which obscured cardinal facets of the church's life, such as its commitment to

- training – all local members of the prayer ministry teams are trained thoroughly and there is a careful selection procedure for the teams working with different churches and denominations
- prayer, with a clear emphasis on intercession and listening to God in order to receive discernment
- outreach; visits to the homeless of Toronto, a notoriously cold city in winter, with food and clothes are a regular feature of the church's life.

Binding these facets together is a passionate servant heart, which has always characterised the ministry of John and Carol. They see their church as a resource centre for God's kingdom so that men and women are captivated afresh by the love of God after a genuine meeting with him.

A consideration of the Toronto Blessing's significance would not be complete, however, without reference to other issues:

1. The whole question of revival.

2. Missionary activity and church planting in Mozambique with Rolland and Heidi Baker.

Let us take these in turn.

1. 'But is it revival?'

This question, in turn, involves two other questions: 'How is the word revival to be defined?' and 'What does revival look like?'

To answer the first of these questions, think of the following careful definitions

'Revival is God coming down in life-stirring
power among His people. It takes place when the
Church is spiritually low and ineffective'
Dr Eifion Evans, see *Fire in the Thatch* and
The Welsh Revival of 1904

'Revival is a visitation from God that restores life to the Church and
produces lasting moral change'
Richard Booker, *How to Prepare for the Coming Revival*
(Destiny Image Publishers, 1990)

'Revival is a movement of the Holy Spirit bringing
about a revival of New Testament Christianity in the
Church of Christ and the related community'
Dr J. Edwin Orr[78]

'Revival is always the action of God. It is not man. It is God pouring
out His Spirit. It is something quite out of the ordinary, something
special, unusual, exceptional'
Dr Martyn Lloyd-Jones, *Revival*

'Revival is God revealing himself to men in awesome
holiness and irresistible power' Arthur Wallis,
In the Day of Thy Power
(Christian Literature Crusade, 1956)

'Revival is a season in the life of the Church when
God causes the normal ministry of the Gospel to surge forward with
extraordinary spiritual power'
Dr Raymond Ortlund[79]

From these quotations it is possible to deduce that revival (1) is
seasonal, not perennial – all revivals, by definition, end; (2)
comes from God, and only from him. Men can end revivals, but
only God can start them. God is sovereign in respect of revival;
(3) is to the church, then to the world, affecting its social and
moral climate in radical ways; (4) is characterised by an intense
sense of God's presence and intimacy; (5) brings both
refreshing and intimacy.

The second question is posed in Dr Mark Stibbe's book,
Times of Refreshing, in which he extrapolates eighteen features
from R.B. Jones' classic work, *Rent Heavens*. Stibbe shows that
revivals

- are always God's initiatives, not man's
- follow pleading to God in prayer
- are intimately connected with the exaltation of Jesus Christ
- are accompanied by extraordinary phenomena
- result in continuous and exuberant praise
- impact the globe, centrifugally
- have a marked centripetal effect (to and from the location of
  revival)
- lead to effective preaching of the gospel
- evoke an acute consciousness of sin
- produce large number of converts
- result in a hunger for the word of God
- lead to a profound unity between Spirit-filled believers
- bring about a remarkable renewal of prayer
- always create a sense of awe at God's holy and pervasive
  presence
- lead people to meet continually in order to encounter God
- produce a much higher level of financial giving
- produce beneficial effects in the wider community
- lead to a sense of the imminence of the Parousia (the return
  of Jesus Christ).

So the crucial consideration now is to identify the criteria fulfilled by the Toronto outpouring. In the author's view, the following distinctives have been present since January 1994.

God's initiative
Whilst John and Carol and Randy Clark too had longed for more spiritual power in their lives and ministries, they had no inner conviction that anything other than routine meetings were about to take place in January 1994. Certainly expectations had been aroused by their trips to Indonesia and Argentina, but this was a far cry from any certainty regarding the outcome of Clark's visit. In fact, they were surprised (and thrilled, of course) by what took place.

Pleading prayer
For a period of at least eighteen months John and Carol had devoted their mornings to intense prayer for a dynamic work of God in their lives and church.

The felt presence of God
This is a feature that thousands of people have commented on, including Lindell Cooley who on his first visit to Toronto felt 'the power of God' sweep over him: 'While everything else seemed so different in the service, I recognised the familiar presence of God. [He] began a deep work of repentance, [pulling] off layer after layer of pride and spiritual arrogance from me. He pulled off religion, so I could embrace relationship with Him.'[80]

John Arnott often refers, in this context to an experiences he had in Israel in 1975 which he sees as truly life-changing: 'I met the love of God in an amazing way. I could not sleep as night after night waves of love washed over me: they were so strong that I thought I would die. God's love was revealed to me that week and I have never been the same since. Truly it was a breakthrough and a formative experience.'

Thousands of converts
At each meeting, unequivocal reference is made to the 'good news' of the gospel, sin, God's love, Jesus' death on the cross,

and the paramount need for men and women to place personal faith and trust in Jesus, as Saviour and as the starting-point of the Christian life. The numbers of converts have been less than Pensacola, with its converts numbering in excess of a hundred and thirty thousand; and less than the Welsh Revival 1904–05 when a hundred thousand people were converted in the first nine months of the revival, but several thousands of converts is a significant number.

Reinvigoration of individual Christians
If only for this facet alone the Toronto Blessing would be significant, and it certainly comes under the umbrella of 'renewal'. The testimonies of such people are not, as has been claimed, fodder for or evidence of the authenticity of the Blessing *per se*, they are the individual responses of people who genuinely feel that God has touched them with a new love for himself, a fresh hunger for the Scriptures, and a new desire for holiness of living. To expect the leaders at TACF to exercise ongoing pastoral responsibility for people from all over the world, is patently impractical if not unreasonable, but John and Carol and their ministry team do advise people to monitor their experience in their local churches at home, in a manner reminiscent of Dr Billy Graham's approach. It is difficult to see what else can be done.

The exaltation of Jesus and the importance of the cross
This is the ultimate litmus paper test of all Christian activity, not just the Toronto Blessing. As G.J. Morgan rightly says in *What is Revival?* (published by Ambassador in 1995), the motivating force behind all outpourings of the Holy Spirit 'must be the Cross of the Lord Jesus Christ. It is the greatest theme in the universe.'

Unusual manifestations of the Spirit
Such manifestations have been witnessed in revivals throughout the ages, the prototype for all revivals being Pentecost. More will be said in the next chapter about the way the leadership at TACF dealt with the phenomena.

The indispensability of the Scriptures
John and Carol have always viewed the Scriptures as the
'bedrock' for everything they do, including the 'comple-
mentarity' of word and Spirit.

A deeper love for God
Individuals and indeed, whole churches, discover a renewal of
their love for God, and worship takes on new meaning – no
longer merely empty ritual. The Bible also 'comes to life' as
'dryness' disappears. This is also the testimony of many, many
people after visiting Toronto or attending Toronto-style
meetings. An outpouring of love to God and humanity
expressed in practical ways is one of the five characteristics of
revival according to Jonathan Edwards in *The Distinguishing
Marks*, alongside which there is an increased sensitivity to the
harmful effects of sin in the lives of Christians.

To these distinctives may be added exuberant praise and
worship. On the other hand, John and Carol accept that the
Toronto Blessing has had only a limited effect in two vital
areas. First it has not impacted the social and moral climate of
the city of Toronto in a general sense. Both the Azusa Street
revival[81] and the Welsh Revival 1904–05 did beneficially affect
the fabric of society; and so too did the more recent Pensacola
revival, although admittedly to a more limited extent. So the
Toronto Blessing is not an 'awakening' when, in Dr J. Edwin
Orr's definition, the community at large takes an interest in the
Christian faith and is affected by its teaching. Second it has not
led to the global revival many anticipated in the early days of
the Blessing. In the fevered and feverish excitement of 1994–96
especially, many people were confident that the greatest
revival in the history of the world was about to occur. It did
not, and the decline of the western church in particular
continues as previously, while the spiritual and moral plight of
western nations is desperate. John and Carol are disappointed
that the Toronto Blessing did not lead to worldwide revival,
but they continue to pray that God will again 'rend the heavens
and come down'.

Analysis

So how finally is the question, 'Is the Toronto Blessing revival?' to be answered? The details alluded to above suggest that it contains elements of refreshing, renewal and revival. Jeremy Sinnott uses this cautious phrase about the Toronto Blessing: 'It is moving towards revival', while David Campbell, a prominent Elim Pentecostal leader in Britain is of the opinion that 'The Toronto Blessing is a renewing movement. In Britain, it has revived the church while, at the same time, exhibiting revival phenomena. It is definite progress towards revival.'[82] In this context Campbell perceives it as a trigger of or a preparation for revival, though he also says that it needs two additional dimensions: a real, desperate, hunger for God, and a more outward evangelistic thrust. To Campbell, therefore, the Toronto Blessing is a renewal to the church primarily, with the added, and valuable, effect of opening men and women up to the Holy Spirit, in all the major Christian denominations; and it is a source of considerable personal satisfaction to him to be associated with John and Carol for their 'unstinting graciousness in the way they have poured themselves out for thousands of churches and individuals across the nations.'

The heart of the matter

The 'essential contribution of the Toronto Blessing,' says Dr Clark Pinnock, 'lies in its spirituality of playful celebration.'[83] With joy and laughter, thousands of people have enjoyed the presence of God which, in turn, has led to an intimate sense of God's love in a robust and energising way. It has revitalised worship and, dare it be said, restored fun to Christianity in a manner that is also consistent with the holiness and otherness of God. Frequently John and Carol use the words 'party' and 'celebration' to pin-point their understanding of the Father heart of God, and alongside this awareness has come repentance, confession, forgiveness and restoration for countless thousands of men and women. Inner healing too is a significant feature of the Toronto Blessing, with deeply ingrained and corrosive sins being removed from people's lives. Such fruit can only be beneficial, and is a firm rebuttal of the criticism that the Blessing is a frivolous and meaningless activity. This sense of personal refreshment can then be offered to other people: it can be given away, not merely as a static thing, but that more fruit can be apparent: with God there is always more.

The Blessing in this sense has nothing whatsoever to do with Toronto – it has everything to do with Father God, it is his Blessing, his nearness is priceless – as Sarah Edwards, wife of Jonathan Edwards stated so memorably: 'I am overwhelmed with His nearness to me and my dearness to Him.' This is why, of course, it has transcended denominational, personal and theological boundaries. An American High Court Judge may well find himself standing next to a reformed alcoholic and drug addict, while a Northern Ireland protestant may be prayed for by a Roman Catholic member of the ministry team. Labels are not important, it's the transforming experience of God that is the key thing, and major conferences at Toronto are attended by people from all denominations: Apostolics, Anglicans, Assemblies of God, Baptists, Brethren, Independent charismatics, Methodists and Salvation Army, to name but a few of the major groupings.

The significance of the Toronto Blessing is both manifold and powerful, but none more so than in Mozambique, to which we now turn.

2. Missionary activity

Mozambique: A downloading of Toronto

At first glance, Toronto and Mozambique could hardly be more different. Toronto is a prosperous, cosmopolitan city with huge social and medical resources whereas Mozambique is one of – if not *the* – most abjectly deprived countries in the world. There grinding poverty is an everyday fact of life for a high percentage of the population, and in the most remote rural areas 40,000 people are served by just one doctor. Hardly surprisingly, ill health is rampant, with the levels of AIDS at epidemic proportions.

What possible link then could there be between the sophisticated city of Toronto and a desperately poor African country? Put briefly, the link is the missionary activity of Rolland and Heidi Baker, founders of Iris Ministries. Rolland's grandfather, H.A. Baker, was a missionary in China for two decades, and he had grown up with an intimate knowledge of missionary work and of revivals. Heidi, an American by birth, had grown up in Laguna Beach, California, where she began ministering at the age of sixteen. In early 1994, Rolland and Heidi were leading a church for homeless people in London where they were also researching for doctoral degrees in systematic theology at King's College, University of London. God though had other plans for them which did not involve cloistered academic study.

On first hearing of the unusual manifestations in Toronto Rolland, in particular, was not particularly impressed: '[I] took almost no interest.' The reason for his lukewarm response was because the reports were consistent with the revival testimonies relayed to him by his grandfather, author of the missionary classic *Visions Beyond the Veil* (published by Sovereign World).

By this time too, and although exhausted after sixteen years missionary activity in China, Hong Kong and Indonesia, both Rolland and Heidi had a passionate desire to serve the poor, the deprived, the homeless and the marginalised members of society, and increasingly they found themselves drawn to Mozambique where two-thirds of the people are illiterate, only 5 per cent have electricity, and where half the children die before the age of five.

In 1995, Rolland arrived in Mozambique for a fortnight's exploratory visit only to be offered a broken-down, totally vandalised orphanage that no one wanted: not the government nor any other care or missionary agency: The Children No One Wanted, as Rolland and Heidi wrote later. Rolland accepted, though the prospects for this work could hardly be more dispiriting or bleak. Soon contending with political corruption as well as looking after the poor and the deprived left Heidi feeling 'deep down bone tired'. At this point Heidi, desperately hungry for God and seriously ill with pneumonia, decided to visit Toronto.

During her first meeting there she had a dramatic encounter with Jesus. In a vision, she saw him surrounded by thousands of children, her initial response being to recoil in horror at the magnitude of the vision, especially when Jesus said: 'Give them to eat. I died so that there would always be enough.'

From that juncture onwards Heidi has never turned away an orphaned, abandoned or dying child, simply because she believes absolutely in the promises Jesus gave her in Toronto. On a subsequent visit to Toronto she was given a second life-transforming vision. She saw a magnificent wedding feast, and heard Jesus speaking to her: 'The feast is about to begin. The poor have not yet been called and my house is not yet full. I want my house to be full.' Later, in 1998, she heard Jesus say that she would have hundreds of churches to take care of.' This vision was both surprising and humorous, as together with Rolland she had only planted four churches in eighteen years of determined and energetic missionary activity.

Six years on from that decisive moment Rolland and Heidi now oversee the work of Iris Ministries amongst thousands of orphans and 6,000 churches in Mozambique.

This story of glorious expansion is comprehensively documented in *There is Always Enough*, published in 2003 by Sovereign World. The three visions Heidi received in Toronto mirror key aspects of the work in Mozambique, and the link between that country and Toronto is not incidental. The first vision assured her that God's supplies are always sufficient. The second reminded her of the church's continuing duty to the poor and the dispossessed, while the third gave a prophetic glimpse into the future and the expansion of the churches God desired in Mozambique. In one sense, these visions were overwhelming, given the perilous nature of life in Mozambique and its ongoing violence and the parlous, almost non-existent, state of their finances. Rolland and Heidi's lives have been threatened with violence and death on more than one occasion, but they have remained true to the heavenly visions God gave Heidi on the carpet at TACF.

One former member of the staff at TACF (Ian Ross) memorably described the work in Mozambique as 'a downloading of Toronto', by which he meant that probably of all the countries in the world affected by the Toronto Blessing, Mozambique has been the most affected through the work of the Bakers. Their experiences in Toronto increased their love for Jesus, sharpened their already existing vision for the poor and the people of Mozambique. The years since 1998 have witnessed an incredible expansion in their work, a burden only possible because of the sublime certainty that they had heard from God clearly and unmistakably.

The challenges confronting them each day are immense. Physical and spiritual hunger abound, and God is constantly enlarging the boundaries of their faith. At no time was this more apparent than during the floods of 2001. Already feeding over six hundred people a day, God's word to Rolland and Heidi was that they should feed 5,000 people, and this with the princely sum of $27.00 in the bank. What transpired was a staggering journey of faith. They

- duly fed 5,000 people each day
- later fed 10,000 people each day
- saw 10,000 people converted to Christianity in a period of just six weeks.

Rolland and Heidi's odyssey of faith goes on unrelentingly in a country where the social fabric is close to collapse because so many health workers, teachers and policemen are dying of AIDS. Whilst not minimising the extent of the task facing them on a daily basis, they know that 'God's power is made perfect in weakness' (see 2 Cor. 12:9), an emphasis western Christianity needs seriously to heed. The move of God in Mozambique is one they have longed for all their lives, it is happening before their very eyes. No other description is appropriate.

The above account shows that the link between Toronto and Mozambique is to be located in the effect of God's powerful presence on Heidi and her responsiveness to the visions he gave her. Together with Rolland and their co-workers, they are translating God's vision into practical, humanitarian and evangelistic outreach in a manner that is both exciting and humbling.

A personal perspective

Writing this book has been both daunting and exciting. Daunting because of the many sharply – and in some cases acrimoniously – divided perspectives offered. It quickly became apparent that many of the Blessing's critics would remain obdurate in opposing everything that it stood for, and nothing would convince them otherwise. This book is most decidedly not an attempt to change people's firmly and, this book assumes, genuinely held convictions. It did seem regrettable though that all too often people opposed what they had only heard about at second or third hand. It was also exciting because, in the words of the Reverend J.A.K. (Sandy) Millar it enabled comparisons to be drawn from 'accounts of early revivals', when God moved dynamically so as to affect whole societies and countries. He commented as follows in an editorial for the *Focus* in-house magazine of Holy Trinity Brompton in September 1994

> People are experiencing the love of God in new ways, finding the acceptance of a loving heavenly Father, discovering deliverance in some cases – growing in their walk with God, their love for the Bible, and being released in a new joy at the same time. It is a sovereign work of God with his people and we are surely grateful for every sign of his grace.

There is nothing so sweet as experiencing the presence of God, as the great revivalist Jonathan Edwards recorded in 1735: 'The town seemed to be full of the presence of God. It was never so full of love, nor of joy, and yet so full of distress, as it was then.'

What then are the central assumptions of this biography? They are that:

1. John and Carol were specifically 'called' of God to lead a movement, the effects of which have been noticed in many countries of the world. A complementary issue is that they were shaped and honed for this task in a number of different ways, including their personal lives and a diverse range of Christian experiences. This shaping is a characteristic they share with

other men and women who have led movements of renewal or revival throughout history. It is not something they emphasise about themselves, but it is clearly apparent to those who have worked with them or been affected by their ministry. There is therefore a distinct 'anointing' on their lives, which has been accompanied by a marked demonstration of the fruit of the Spirit in their lives in general, not just when ministering in a public setting; and this unity of function and character has earned respect and affection in abundant measures. The Christian community can be a critical one, but John and Carol are almost unique in the way they have avoided (for the most part) personal censure or obloquy. They are ordinary people in the hands of an extraordinary and supernatural God.

2. The Toronto Blessing is essentially a source of refreshment to the church, by reminding it that Father God wishes to enter into an intimate bond with his people which is based not on performance but on relationship. Alongside this refreshment has been cleansing and re-equipping for service. Worship, both individual and public, is central to the very fabric of the 'Toronto Blessing', as the many 'love songs' emanating from it so eloquently attest. Put slightly differently, the river of God has elevated countless thousands of people to new levels of love, forgiveness and healing. In the nineteenth century, F.B. Meyer wrote this: 'The river of God flows on in its glorious fullness, though the professing church has removed from its banks, and is creating a new settlement on the edge of the desert. How disastrous is this experiment.'[84] The 'Toronto Blessing' illustrates what happens when the church comes back from 'the edge of the desert' as guided and directed by the Holy Spirit: there is a recovery of love, faith, humility and, dare it be said, fun – God, after all, gives the best parties.

3. The Toronto Blessing is not primarily about the manifestations of the Spirit. It really does not matter at all whether people fall over, raise their hands, laugh uncontrollably or indeed quietly, lie on the floor for short or extended periods of time, or even dance. What does matter, and profoundly too, is that men and women have a loving,

ennobling relationship with God and are prepared and eager to allow him to transform their lives in radical and lasting ways.

4. The Toronto Blessing is a rousing call to persevere in prayer, so that God's magnificent promises become a reality in the lives of individuals and the church as a corporate body. John and Carol pray unceasingly for the personal revival which bestows the power, in the words of Richard Bieber, in *Set Our Hearts On Fire* (Vine Books, 1998), 'to live in this world as servants of God and of each other. The Spirit who lives in us is the Spirit of servanthood. He imparts to us the very mind of Christ'; and also for the global revival which will show to a hostile and deeply cynical world the irresistible power of God's kingdom. Such a revival (defined by one commentator as 'a visitation from God that renews the life of the church and produces lasting moral change'), they insist, can be prepared for so that 'God will send it in response to our desire and willingness to receive it' (Richard Booker, in *How To Prepare For The Coming Revival*, Destiny Image Publishers, 1990, p.3). The Toronto Blessing is most certainly not an end in itself, but it is an encouragement to people who presently struggle with a tepid awareness of God's love, with fear, with a sense of worthlessness, with a lack of resolve to obey God's word, or simply with the distractions of everyday living, that God has so much more for them than has previously been experienced. It is a thrilling reminder that God's heart is passionate about us as people, and is a motivator to be 'Jesus-centred' individuals who help others into God's holy presence as opposed to being a barrier. Ultimately the significance of the 'Toronto Blessing' is that Christians need not slumber along in a state of mediocrity, rather that they can enjoy the limitless resources of God each and every day of their lives. They can know and enjoy the immediate presence of God, bringing freshness instead of staleness, forgiveness instead of bitterness, freedom instead of enslavement, and hope instead of despair. What a wonderful vision for the twenty-first century.

Chapter Six
Looking back, looking forward

A total surprise

The advent of the Toronto Blessing began with dramatic abruptness, surprising not only John and Carol and Randy Clark, but also staff members at TACF. Mary-Audrey Raycroft was taking a class in an adjoining room to the main auditorium and when she heard the noise, decided to investigate. As she opened the door leading to the sanctuary, she says 'she was knocked to the floor'. After a little while, she crawled into the room, but couldn't see anyone apart from a few people standing at the front. So where was the noise coming from? It was at this point that she realised that 'all the people were down on the floor between the rows of chairs'. It took some time for her to comprehend what was happening: 'As the scene registered, I went numb from my jaw up to my eyelids – I was struck dumb. The crowd was stunned as the Holy Spirit fell in the room. We were flabbergasted – without a lot of hype, almost without exception, everyone had been powerfully impacted by what we instantly knew could only be God. We had expected a special meeting, but this was a total surprise.' Eleven years on, that sense of amazement remains clearly focused in her memory.

One of those people in the front row was Connie Sinnott. She had just said to Carol Arnott, 'I want something so real that I know it's him – not something I've made up in my mind or warm and nice feelings. At that point one of Randy's ministry team, mistakenly thinking that Connie had come up for prayer, laid hands on her and as soon as she did Connie says: 'I felt tingling in my lips which rapidly spread to my whole face, it felt like dental freezing. It lasted for four hours, and as I was asking God what it was all about, he reminded me of my earlier conversation with Carol.'

John and Carol Arnott were equally surprised, not least when someone they knew well, Joanne Radke, fell to the floor and was 'stuck there', unable to move a muscle. The friends she was supposed to go out with afterwards simply left her there, not quite being able to understand why she was laughing so uproariously. Reflecting later on that first weekend of the Toronto Blessing (*Spread the Fire*, February 1999), John says that he had often wondered about the metaphors used to describe the Holy Spirit in the Scriptures: fire, oil, wind, spirit, rain, river, but was perplexed: 'I often thought about how ineffective the Western Church had become, and particularly, how ineffective my own ministry was.' He adds: 'I believed that the Holy Spirit was powerful, but it's one thing to have information based on history and theology and quite another to experience Him.' In fact, surprise is too tepid a word to describe John and Carol's reactions. They were quite simply amazed, because as John wrote later in the same article, 'I watched the River of God flow from one to another in utter amazement. The anointing was so contagious. Everyone it touched came alive to the presence of God.' 'We didn't want to miss a thing,' says Mary-Audrey Raycroft, 'even though the meetings went on [each night] into the early hours of the following morning.'

The Long Haul

By the end of the third week, John and Carol had seen more men and women converted than in all their previous years of ministry. They were overwhelmed, and constantly wondered, how long would this go on? At this stage Carol was given a vision of heaven and the city of God, ending with a strong exhortation from the Lord to be like the wise virgins in Matthew 25, to buy the oil of the Holy Spirit that was being so freely dispensed. A staff meeting was called, at which John indicated that they were in for the long haul. Let John himself explain in words that get to the very essence of the Toronto Blessing, and explain also why it has carried on for so long

> The staff looked at me like I was crazy. We were already tired after three weeks of meetings every single night. How could we go on for months or even years? There was something about the powerful presence of the Holy Spirit that we were quickly learning. You don't have him; he has you. He has come to take control. I suppose that is why I felt so overwhelmed. We felt as if we were all being swept downstream in a wonderful river of life. I remember crying out, 'God, what do I do?' He spoke clearly saying, 'Don't package this, don't market this, don't try to exploit this to grow your own ministry, but just give it away.'

Alongside the element of surprise was another distinct feeling, expressed simply by John as follows: 'In the beginning we were all like excited children just enjoying the river of God.' They are emphatic on two aspects of the Holy Spirit's presence. First he always exalts and, second, he always works within the boundaries of the Scriptures.

For the first few months John and Carol lived each day as if it would be the 'last' day of the Spirit's powerful presence and transforming power at TACF and they called a host of friends to share the good news with them. In reality, they were afraid it would not last and they didn't want anyone to miss out on what God was doing. They maintained a genuinely wondering 'innocence' at the Spirit's gracious operation; and still do to this day. John and Carol clearly understood that it was all of God's grace, not of them, and for which they could not take any credit, not that they wished to do so. Eleven years on John and Carol are as balanced and as grounded in the Scriptures as they have always been, and still exulting in the work of the Spirit.

Imbalances

All periods of renewal or revival are something of a mixed blessing, as none of them, as Frank Damazio carefully observes in *Seasons of Revival*, 'will offer a completely pure river where everything that is happening [is] a pure product of the Holy Spirit'. Put slightly differently, mistakes are made and imbalances occur in all outpourings of the Holy Spirit.

In retrospect, it is clear that the Toronto Blessing did not

- provide enough theological under-girding of the normative New Testament experience of the baptism of the Spirit
- distinguish sufficiently between certain phenomena. John and Carol defended the comparatively rare instances of barking/howling and other animal noises that occurred. This gave some observers a great opportunity for criticism. A few people also roared, including famously Bishop David Pytches, but it might have been wiser, and certainly less contentious, not to attempt a theological under-girding of the animal noises which are not, in any case what the Toronto Blessing is primarily about. Occasionally it's best to say: 'we don't know'
- offer a clear explanation of the concept of mission. In this context, the lack of an evangelist on the staff of TACF to explain the Blessing from an evangelistic perspective was regrettable
- sufficiently explain, at least in its early stages, its true nature, intent and purpose: to pour water on hardened, dry ground. Prejudices have not been broken up and the Toronto Blessing has not fulfilled its ultimate goal of preparing the church for global revival and mission. On the other hand, it did renew the church especially in terms of the presence of God and the paramount need for both theology and practice
- place sufficient emphasis on the testing of the spirits. The ability to distinguish between the spirits (1 Cor. 12:10) is vitally important where supernatural spiritual activity is concerned.

In addition, it is also clear that several of the arguments put forward by proponents of the Toronto Blessing were not always helpful. The first of these was the early invoking of Jonathan Edwards to support the unusual phenomena witnessed in the meetings, especially the physical phenomena. Critics and the sceptics heartily disapproved of the noise and the manifestations, and the appeals to Edwards did not satisfy them. Edwards was aware that sceptics would dismiss the physical phenomena as irrational religious behaviour, commenting ironically as follows: 'If such things are enthusiasm and the fruits of a distempered brain, let my brain be evermore possessed of that happy distemper. If this be distraction, I pray God that the whole world of mankind be seized with this benign, meek, beneficent, beautiful, glorious distraction.' But he also insisted that the manifestations do not indicate either positively or negatively about the authenticity of the spiritual experience: 'A work is not to be judged by any effects on the bodies of men, such as tears, trembling, groans, loud outcries, agonies of body, or the failing of bodily strength.' In the event, opponents of the Toronto Blessing became fixated on the physical manifestations while tending, at the same time, to ignore what was the primary thrust of the outpouring: the exaltation of Jesus, the renewal of Christians and the church, leading to a spirit of forgiveness, humility, and increased longings for holiness.

The second unhelpful argument to approve of the Toronto Blessing was in terms of the so-called 'Gamaliel principle', which is outlined in Acts 5:38: 'for if this counsel or this work be of men, it will come to naught' (KJV). Some, including the British leader of the Salvation Army and Dr Mark Stibbe accepted this as a godly response to the Blessing, while other equally prominent British Christians (such as Peter Masters, John Stott and Tom Smail) did not consider it to be a reliable or indeed adequate Christian response. The invoking of this principle has led to a great deal of constructive theological and academic debate (as in *The Mark of the Spirit?*), but for the ordinary reader the weakest point of the Gamaliel principle is that it would have to be applied to other religions like Islam or Buddhism, whereas the Toronto Blessing is palpably a Christian movement.

A third unhelpful proposition on the part of proponents of the Toronto Blessing was to place an apprehension of it on an equal footing with the disciples' apprehension of Pentecost: the so-called 'This-is-That Hermeneutics'. Mark Smith makes the valid observation that the disciples were explicitly told by Jesus to wait in Jerusalem for the baptism of the Holy Spirit, the promise of the Father (Acts 1:4,5). Consequently, as Smith says, 'when they experienced Pentecost, they had direct teaching from Jesus to explain it. So, while Peter had good reason to say that the Pentecost experience was promised by God and so the fulfilment of the Scriptures, we do not have good reason to do the same with the "Toronto Blessing".'[85] It might have been more appropriate for supporters of the Blessing to speak, not in terms of fulfilment, with its implication of a reduplicated experience, but in terms of an experience of the same order, belonging to the same category. Diversity of experience is surely the significance here rather than one experience being a replica of the other.

Why are your critics so angry?

John and Carol were deeply puzzled by the reactions of some people, and he remains disconcerted by a question one reporter put to him (*Spread the Fire*, December 1999): 'Why are your critics so angry?' He responded to the question like this

> We have not changed our order of service. We have the same orthodox statement of faith. Lives are being saved and transformed supernaturally. I want to say to them, 'If you simply don't like the way we do things, then stay away, or come up with a better way of evangelising your city and community, but please don't criticise brothers who believe the very same statement of faith that you do, and by all means, don't attribute the works of the Holy Spirit to the devil.' It amazes me at how quickly some do just that. We needn't be surprised when we don't understand everything God does.

He is frequently asked if he would do anything differently, to which he responds by saying this: 'I believe I would have one of our team dedicated to responding to criticism.' He says this because so many people have been frightened away from the Toronto Blessing.

Six years on from his words quoted above, it seems most unlikely that such an initiative – responding to criticism – would have the desired effect because of the impasse that exists between the defenders and the detractors of the Toronto Blessing. In this context John and Carol wisely take refuge in the instructions of Jesus in Matthew 7:16–18: 'By their fruit you will recognise them. . . . A good tree cannot bear bad fruit, and a bad tree cannot bear good fruit.' (NIV) They totally accept that the lasting impact of the Toronto Blessing has yet to be determined – that will be the rôle of theologians and church historians in years to come, but meanwhile reference may be made to the way in which men, women and also children have been deeply affected by what John calls 'this wonderful infilling of the Holy Spirit', and he asks rhetorically: 'How do you put a value on a life transformed forever by the power of God?'

A fascinating aspect of the Arnotts response to the question of 'fruit' in people's lives is that they accepted Dr Margaret Poloma's suggestion that she should carry out a sociological survey of a test group of people who had been to Toronto (see End Notes: 34). The value of such a survey could provide, in Dr Poloma's words, 'a tool to determine whether individuals perceive their lives to be better as a result of the [Toronto Blessing], whether their relationships with family and friends have changed, and whether their experiences have empowered them to reach out to others in the larger community.' Such a methodology leaves the reader to make the judgement concerning whether the 'fruit' produced by the Toronto Blessing is good or bad (see Matthew 7:16–18 above). Again in Dr Poloma's words, 'It offers a way to break the deadlock between defenders and critics of the Renewal by presenting evidence about the impact the Toronto Blessing is having in the lives of thousands of people who have tasted of its fruit and judged it to be good.'

The empirical evidence collected was then analysed under a number of different headings, including

- Refreshing through revelations of God's love
- Holiness, wholeness and healing
- Repentance and Forgiveness
- Emotional, Mental and Physical Healing
- Evangelism and Outreach
- Social Relations (with wives and husbands).

Dr Poloma concluded that 'the experiential spirituality reflected in this [sociological] study is one that is balanced: a healthy sense of personal sin in the face of God's holiness, a willingness to forgive and to be forgiven, and an ability to accept God's love and the love of others.' She also concluded that the Toronto Blessing is not essentially about physical manifestations, rather it is 'about satisfying the desire of the human heart. It is about human beings encountering a God of love who empowers them to share what they have been given.' It is, as John and Carol teach, a life-transforming experience that affects individuals, churches and societies. It is what Dr Poloma calls 'the illuminative love of God', which she considers to be 'the central message of the Toronto Blessing'. They talk about such a transformation as a 'life-changing love affair with Jesus', and in *Keep The Fire* (p.143) John cites the example of a lady from England who had been a Christian for more than twenty years. Her main desire in visiting Toronto was to 'know' how much Jesus loved her. Of course, she knew theologically and theoretically that Jesus loved her, but when she said that to someone else, 'it barely convinced me, let alone them.' At Toronto, she experienced the love and intimacy of Jesus in a mind-blowing way and, significantly, in a way that has lasted: 'Even on my own, I sense Jesus with me in a most beautiful way.'

But it is not love at the expense of holiness, and John and Carol emphasise that holiness is not peripheral; it is absolutely central to the whole of our Christian lives, and they heartily endorse the words of P.T. Forsyth from the nineteenth century: 'Sin is but the defiance of God's holiness, grace is but its action upon sin, the cross is but its victory, and faith is but its worship.'[86] Holiness, as they see it combines the idea of God's majesty (or transcendence) and the need for Christians to regulate their lives so as to conform to his character and directives.

'Something to give your life for'

Reflecting on the rise and spread of the Toronto Blessing raises another important consideration; its leadership and pastoral management. Clearly problems of attention-seeking or the pursuit of the sensational by some people have arisen, the pursuit of the 'experiences' in and of themselves, and John and Carol have striven determinedly to protect what God is doing from the misguided behaviour of such people. They are not afraid (particularly John) to exercise discipline when it is required. They have also, from time to time, been disappointed by the responses of some of those closely associated with them: again, in such instances, appropriate measures have been taken, although from their perspective the problems encountered have been 'minimal' compared with the over-whelming testimonies of God's goodness. On the other hand, they have been careful to exercise biblically based restraints, constantly encouraging their church and visitors to TACF to meditate upon the Scriptures and to submit their lives actively to the enlightenment of the word of God and the ongoing influence of the Holy Spirit. So godliness and practical obedience are frequently stressed in their preaching and teaching.

The events of January 1994 catapulted John and Carol into a much wider form of leadership than they had known previously which, in turn, meant facing a more insistent and more demanding spotlight. How did they cope with the enormous demands on their time and, equally crucially, their energies?

The starting-point is their excitement at, and appreciation of, what was happening before their eyes. John often says that the Toronto Blessing (or more preferably the Father's Blessing) is something to die for. By this he means that his desire for God to move in a new way has been amply and thrillingly fulfilled. Words like 'thrilled', 'amazed', and 'overwhelmed' barely do justice to the enormous sense of privilege they feel at God's call to both a local and a global ministry. Exhausted they often are, but they would not swap their present lifestyle for their lives prior to January 1994. In 1993, for example, and despite the prophecies of friends such as Marc Dupont and Stacey Campbell that 'more' was on the way, John in particular had almost given up believing that a fresh move of God was on the way, and certainly not imminent. John and Carol's hunger for God overtook their fears and they responded wholeheartedly to the fullness of the Holy Spirit demonstrated so dynamically in the meetings led by Randy Clark. Their enthusiasm could not be contained, and the Internet began carrying reports across the world about events in a 400-seat building at the end of a runway. Soon, of course, this building was inadequate to accommodate the crowds that came.

Another possible explanation has to do with the people John and Carol Arnott were then and are now. In other words, their leadership reflected their 'character' and motivation, the key to which is found in an article John wrote in 1999: 'You who are seeking more of [Jesus] realise that He values character every bit as much as giftedness.' He then adds this cautionary comment: 'If you seek [Jesus] because you love Him, and not for your own agenda's sake to be successful or noticed, you will not go wrong.' So the Toronto Blessing, in their view, is not something to be exploited in a pastoral or financial sense. It is, however, something to be welcomed and enjoyed; and this is what John and Carol have done for over eleven years. Some of their main qualities as people have been discussed earlier in the book, but it is vitally important to perceive their 'character' in the mosaic that is the Toronto Blessing.

John and Carol Arnott are genuinely gentle people who love God with all their hearts, and this has been an inspiration to many, many people in different parts of the world. Determined to trust God through everything, they are also determined to allow the Holy Spirit to have his way in their lives. 'Through their ministry,' says Derek Brown, of KC 21 (formerly The King's Church), Aldershot, England, 'a definite prophetic statement is being made regarding what God wants to do in terms of Christian identity, the Father heart of God, and the presence of the Holy Spirit. In the Toronto Blessing, which I consider to be a genuine move of God, God is indicating what sort of church he's looking for. In particular, God is showing that in the body of Christ, Spirit-filled ministry is not just with the professionals; and he wants to equip all the saints for the works of service.' It is instructive to emphasise Brown's point about all the saints being equipped for service because John has actively given women a prominent place in public meetings in a manner reminiscent of Evan Roberts in the 1904–05 revival in Wales.

The Arnotts are worshippers, and Jeremy Sinnott fondly recalls John using an auto-harp to lead worship when they planted their first church in Stratford. He didn't have a particularly keen ear for the cadences of music, but he did want to praise and worship God with his whole being. Worship has always been a central thrust at TACF too, while Carol, says Jeremy Sinnott, 'taught him how to worship'. Much of the worship is occupied with 'love songs', exalting Jesus, and all in a gentle and unhurried way. John and Carol reiterate the importance of worship wherever they minister, stressing the need to listen to what the Holy Spirit is saying through it. Intimacy in worship is a key to understanding the Toronto Blessing.

The manner of their preaching flows from the platforms of prayer and worship in their lives. They are not interested in impressing other people, they simply give what God has given to them. Inevitably though, their personalities shine through – Carol is more outgoing, while John's preaching has an understated eloquence. Ideas do not interest them especially because they just want to get on with God's work. Their piety is manifest to all who meet them, but alongside this, particularly in John's administrative rôles, is a great deal of practical common sense. This was illustrated when men and women from Toronto started itinerating around the world. He established a set minimum fee per day or per meeting to ensure that basic needs were met. This sensible strategy enabled them to 'carry' the Blessing without the burden of financial pressures – it also meant that they (the itinerants) could go to poverty-stricken nations and prisons where, obviously, no remuneration would be forthcoming. There is an additional aspect to his common-sense arrangements: he ensured that those in itinerating ministries did not profit in an extravagant manner. In this way too, John was encouraging local churches to accept their responsibility in a financial sense. The same financial rectitude or accountability is apparent in the organisation of TACF and its permanent staff.

In this way John models the whole idea of responsible and godly leadership. He is not afraid to learn from other people in areas where he is not an expert. Neither John nor Carol consider themselves to 'have arrived', and they regard themselves as some of 'God's broken leaders'; and it is not a surprise that God has brought countless numbers of 'broken people' to TACF and the conferences, especially the 'Healing Life's Hurts' conference. They feel honoured to be leaders in God's kingdom, and accept the burden of extensive travelling and staying in different hotels as part and parcel of that honour. An essential aspect of leadership is to encourage leadership potential in other men and women and this is a notable achievement in their lives. Colin Dye refers to them as 'affirming, patient, loving people, in whom the fruit of the Spirit is apparent in their daily lives.' Many people interviewed for this book (with their own significant ministries) referred to the encouragement they have received from the Arnotts, not least when going through times of difficulty, the result being refreshment: 'John and Carol,' says Colin Dye, 'have the capacity to lift people up.' David Campbell (senior pastor at the City Church in St Albans) views them as 'homely people with a capacity for friendship. They make people comfortable, with an unshockable love and acceptance; and they are prepared to listen to people who nurture different views from themselves.' Campbell also refers to them as 'disarming people, without guile, but possessed of enormous wisdom'. John and Carol are easy-going though not naïve people, and TACF is an organised church with a structured staff.

A daily part of leadership is to face disappointments and difficulties, and John and Carol have had their share of these too. Not only those churches which enthusiastically embraced the Toronto Blessing initially and then drifted back to 'safer' programmes, but more particularly the split with the Vineyard churches in 1995. Looking back, they both view the separation as a critical moment in the life of the Toronto Blessing and, presumably, their own leadership of it. They remain convinced, however, that it enabled them to pursue the vision God had given to them, and this takes precedence over any personal feelings of hurt that they may have experienced at that time. Facing personal criticism is also something leaders have to do, and John has had to endure the wild, unsubstantiated strictures. In Hank Hanegraaff's book, *Counterfeit Revival*,[87] Hanegraaff's methodology produces what Dr Michael Brown[88] calls 'an extreme prosperity quote' from one of Hinn's sermons, mentioning in passing that Hinn 'had a profound impact on such Counterfeit Revival leaders as John Arnott', so by association alleges that John Arnott too must hold to such teaching. There are two things wrong with Hanegraaff's assertion: Hinn's influence on John is personal and certainly not profound, while John could hardly be described as a devotee of prosperity teaching. The criticism is referred to here only to show some of the pressures endured by John and Carol over the past eleven years.

What's next?

Eleven years on from January 1994 John and Carol are as balanced and as grounded in their ministry as they ever were, still enjoying the work of the Holy Spirit and his transforming power, still eager to elevate others to leadership, still hungry for the presence of God. The question that they are most insistently asked in terms of the future is this: 'What's next?' The short answer they invariably give is: 'What else is there?' This slightly tongue-in-cheek response reflects their gratitude for and enjoyment of the experiences the Holy Spirit has guided them into since January 1994. It does not imply any smug sense of self-satisfaction or any proud apprehension that they 'have arrived' as Christian leaders. It does though express their genuine conviction that they are currently involved in 'the' work God has called them to fulfil. John and Carol are convinced that, in January 1994, they were called by God to lead a particular work, although at that time they did not consider themselves to be 'qualified' for it. A cryptic one-liner perhaps best expresses what has happened: God does not call those who are qualified, he qualifies those who are called. This book's assumption is that this has happened in John and Carol's lives and ministry.

The Arnotts are frequently asked, 'Will it ever end?' John's immediate and heart-felt response is: 'I pray it will end only in the glorious return of our Lord Jesus Christ.' Meanwhile, they will continue to

- pursue the promptings of the Holy Spirit
- stay in the flow of the river of God's blessing
- pastor the local church in Toronto
- oversee the work of 'Partners in Harvest', giving advice and direction as required
- lead the conferences at TACF.

In all of these activities they will endeavour, as they have always done, to walk in God's love and give it away to Toronto, Canada and the world.

Endnotes

[1] Dr Mark Stibbe, *Times of Refreshing: A Practical Theology of Revival For Today* (Marshall Pickering, 1985), especially page 62 ff. and Dr Mark Stibbe, *Revival* (Monarch Books, 1988).

[2] In conversation with the author.

[3] Sub-titled, *Thinking Through The Toronto Phenomenon*, it was published by Hodder & Stoughton in 1995.

[4] Recollections published in *Spread the Fire* (December 1998), pp. 17–19.

[5] Published in 2001.

[6] Quoted at length in D. Hilborn (ed.) *'Toronto' in Perspective* (ACUTE, 2001), p. 16.

[7] Mike Fearon, *A Breath of Fresh Air* (Eagle, 1994), p. 251.

[8] *By Their Fruits: The Lasting Impact of Toronto in the UK* (with a Foreword by John Arnott) (Word Publishing, 2001), p. 171.

[9] Source: *The Quotable Tozer*, published by Christian Publications, Pennsylvania, 1994.

[10] For details of original publishers, readers should consult: *The Works of Jonathan Edwards*, Volume 4 (New Haven: Yale University Press, 1972). See also: *Jonathan Edwards on Revival* (Banner of Truth, 1984) and *Jonathan Edwards: A New Biography* (Carlisle PA: Banner of Truth, 1987).

[11] Dr Martyn Lloyd-Jones, *Revival* (Marshall Pickering, 1986).

[12] *HTB in Focus*, 10 July 1994.

[13] See Chapter Five for fuller, more comprehensive details.

[14] In conversation with the author in 2003 and 2004.

[15] See also Chapter Four.

[16] Published by Destiny Image, 1999.

[17] John's daughter uses precisely the same word about her father.

[18] Compare the apostle Paul's words in 1 Corinthians 2:2-5.

[19] See Desmond Pickering, *The Great Evangelists* (Marshall Pickering, 1986) and Albert W. Edsor, *Set Your House In Order* (New Wine Press, 1989).

[20] These quotes were in a manuscript account sent to the author by Al MacDonald, associate pastor at TACF.

[21] I.D.E. Thomas *God's Harvest* (Gwasg Bryntirion Press, revised edn., 1997).

[22] Quoted from the author's article in *The Impact of Toronto* published by Monarch in 1995.

[23] Ken and Lois Gott, *The Sunderland Refreshing* (Hodder & Stoughton, 1995), pp. 17,18.

[24] Gott, ibid., p. 122.

[25] Eifion Evans, *Fire in the Thatch* (Evangelical Press of Wales, 1996), p. 10.

[26] Based on recollections published in *Spread the Fire* magazine for 1995.

[27] Based on recollections published in *Spread the Fire* magazine for 1995.

[28] In *Spread the Fire* magazine, February 1999.

[29] See Dr Martyn Lloyd-Jones, ibid., p. 47.

[30] See Dr Martyn Lloyd-Jones, ibid., p. 142.

[31] Opinions expressed in D. Hilborn (ed.) *'Toronto' in Perspective* (ACUTE, 2001)

[32] Opinions expressed in D. Hilborn.

[33] Opinions expressed in D. Hilborn.

[34] Quoted from *By Their Fruit: A Sociological Assessment of the Toronto Blessing* (25th annual meeting of the Society for Pentecostal Studies, Wycliffe College, Toronto, On. 1996).

[35] Opinions expressed in D. Hilborn.

[36] See Hilborn, ibid., p. 10.

[37] Randy Clark, *Lighting Fires* (Charisma House, 1998), p. 100.

[38] In conversation with the author in 2003 and 2004.

[39] Quoted in *Revival* by Brian Edwards (Evangelical Press, 1990). See also B.P. Jones *An Instrument of Revival: The Complete Life of Evan Roberts 1878–1951* (South Plainfield, NJ: Bridge Publishing, 1995)

and Eifion Evans, *The Welsh Revival of 1904* (Evangelical Press of Wales, 1969).

⁴⁰ Brian Edwards, *Revival: A people saturated with God.* (Evangelical Press, 1990).

⁴¹ Part of his famous prayer, quoted in *Revival* by Brian Edwards and elsewhere.

⁴² See Clare George Weakley Jr (ed.), *The Nature of Revival* (Bethany House Publishers, 1987).

⁴³ See Robert E. Coleman (ed.), *The Heart of Wesley's Journal* (Labarum Press Ltd., 1979).

⁴⁴ See *By Their Fruits*, pp. 125–131.

⁴⁵ See *By Their Fruits* p. 46.

⁴⁶ Jeff Lucas, *Grace Choices* (Authentic Media, 2004), p. 108.

⁴⁷ (Gen. ed. John Arnott), *Experience the Blessing* (Renew Books, 2000).

⁴⁸ John Arnott, *The Importance of Forgiveness* (Sovereign World, 1997), p. 93.

⁴⁹ *Experience the Blessing,* p. 15.

⁵⁰ R.B. Jones, *Rent Heavens* (Pioneer Mission, 1931), p. 51 ff.

⁵¹ Clifford Hill and others, *Blessing the Church?* (Eagle, 1995), p. 60.

⁵² Quoted at length in Frank Damazio, *Seasons of Revival* (BT Publishing, 1996) pp. 102–103.

⁵³ Opinions culled from *By Their Fruits.*

⁵⁴ Opinions culled from *By Their Fruits.*

⁵⁵ Opinions culled from *By Their Fruits.*

⁵⁶ Opinions culled from *By Their Fruits.*

⁵⁷ *Experience the Blessing,* p. 45.

⁵⁸ See Damazio, ibid., pp. 165–176.

⁵⁹ See Damazio, ibid., pp. 165–176.

⁶⁰ See Dr Martyn Lloyd-Jones, ibid., p. 100.

⁶¹ Famous Campbell quote author found in one of his unpublished sermons, but see also Duncan Campbell, *The Price and Power of Revival* (Scripture Illustrations Ltd, 1956).

⁶² Duncan Campbell, *The Price and Power of Revival,* pp. 36,37.

⁶³ See Ken and Lois Gott, *The Sunderland Refreshing,* ibid.

⁶⁴ *Experience the Blessing,* p. 87.

⁶⁵ See *By Their Fruits* pp. 147–165.

⁶⁶ John Armstrong, *When God Moves* (Harvest House Publishers, 1998), p. 235.

⁶⁷ See Damazio, ibid., p. 155.

[68] Opinions quoted in Hilborn, pp. 14–15.

[69] Opinions quoted in Hilborn, pp. 14–15.

[70] See Hilborn, pp. 35–63.

[71] D. Pawson, *Is The 'Blessing' Biblical?* (Hodder & Stoughton, 1995), p. 80.

[72] R.B. Jones, ibid., p. 47.

[73] *Experience the Blessing*, p. 139.

[74] *Experience the Blessing*, p. 151.

[75] John Kilpatrick, *Feast of Fire* (Marshall Pickering, 1995).

[76] Melinda Fish, article in *Spread the Fire* for December 1998.

[77] *Joy Unspeakable*, (Eastbourne: Kingsway Publications, 1984).

[78] Taken from website on revival.

[79] Taken from website on revival.

[80] *A Touch of Glory* (Destiny Image Publishers, 1997).

[81] This revival of 1906, located in a run-down area of Los Angeles, propelled Pentecostals and Pentecostal beliefs into worldwide expansion. Coming almost immediately after renewals in Wales and Korea, it belonged to what one commentator (Dr J. Edwin Orr) has described as the most extensive evangelical awakening of all time – quote from *Rivers of Revival*, by N.T. Anderson and E.L. Towns (Regal, 1997).

[82] In private conversation with the author.

[83] See his Foreword to *Experience the Blessing*, pp. 3–7.

[84] Quoted by Sandy Miller in article alluded to in the text above.

[85] Lloyd Peterson (ed.), *The Mark of the Spirit?* (Paternoster Press, 1998), p. 60.

[86] Quoted in John Armstrong, *When God Moves*.

[87] Hank Hanegraaff, *Counterfeit Revival: Looking for God in All the Wrong Places* (Dallas: Ward, 1997).

[88] Dr Michael Brown, *Let No One Deceive You* (Revival Press, 1997).